American Badge Betrayed

The toxic reality of police corruption and discrimination

Robert E. Alvarez

 ISBN (Print) 978-1-48359-007-3 (Ebook) 978-1-48359-008-0

Table of Contents

About the Author

Robert E. Alvarez is a decorated Hispanic officer who retired from the Lowell, Massachusetts police after 24 years of service. Throughout his career he held positions as a SWAT team leader and was an instructor of several disciplines. His story is one of a 16 year fight to clear his name that entails detailed battles against police corruption at the highest levels.

The warrior punishes those

who believe themselves beyond

the reach of justice

"High Sparrow" (Game of Thrones)

Foreword

I never had any intentions of writing this book. I thought it would be too difficult and I thought no one would be interested in hearing my story. Yet for some reason, over the years and throughout all the incidents, I continued to keep documentation and take notes. I don't know why I did this, I just did. The catalyst for actually sitting down and writing my story was the news that a movie was going to be made about the marathon bombing in Boston and Ed Davis would be a major part of it, portrayed as a hero. I could tolerate the hypocrisy no longer. I felt an obligation to tell the truth about the extensive corruption in the Lowell Police Department and the truth about the conduct of several of the police chiefs and command staff there.

A lot of the information presented in this book is authenticated with supporting documentation, but some of the information is secondhand, without documentation because it is knowledge that I received directly through what would be considered hearsay in a court of law. Some of the dialogue may not be exact because it is a first-hand account based on my memory. I have done my best to remember the dialogue to the best of my knowledge.

All I have is my story, my experience, and my perception. What you do with that is up to you. I don't know if anyone will read this or if it will make any difference, but this is my last shot. While all other efforts have failed, my last resort is to write this book, exercising the ability to utilize the first amendment from the U.S. Constitution that I swore to defend forty years ago.

Introduction

These are the ballistic vests I wore every day for 24 years. Each vest had a service life of approximately six years. I always had a national ensign sewn over the chest plate that covered my heart. That flag was my flag. It served as a personal symbol of the principles I tried to honor and live by. To me, the flag embodied the whole purpose of wearing the armor and going out on the street. There was a flag on the sleeve of the uniform, but I felt it was just a decoration of the police department I worked for. Over the years I found most cops couldn't give a damn about the flag on the uniform, or the oath we all swore to, for that matter. The flag on my vest was for my own personal integrity.

Once, another cop (who always displayed shamrocks on his costume) saw the flag on my vest and asked, "What the hell is that for?" If you have to ask, then you'll never understand the answer. My white vest on the left was the one I wore first in 1987. This was long before 9/11 when patriotism became a fad. Flags on body armor are pretty commonplace now, just like the sleeve flag. Anybody can wear it. It's another thing to live by it.

One cannot truly understand the police culture unless they are fully immersed in it as an officer themselves. An observer looking in from the outside will not be able to comprehend the convoluted matrix that is the police method of operation. If they can, it will take years to grasp the concepts of this esoteric organization. The public has never had the ability to understand the mindset that police officers have. Blatant police misconduct is frequently deemed as justifiable by politicians and leaders in law enforcement. The defense is often steeped in semantics with an elusive legal angle to support the justification. They present their flimsy defense to the public, which leaves citizens bewildered as the excuses defy human logic.

The way events are reported through the media seem only to further baffle one's ability to understand. The citizens who observe clearly and unequivocally unjustifiable actions are presented with the same disingenuous excuses: "this is police procedure" or "the officer feared for his life". The abundance of raw iPhone videos capturing police misconduct cannot be refuted, yet police command staff and district attorney's continue to fall back to those previously utilized excuses that have always worked in the past. But the viewers of these videos are no longer dissuaded by these simple excuses anymore. How did we get to the point of justifying the execution of unarmed, non-threatening citizens? Presently, the police are having a much harder time explaining away and justifying police criminal conduct as a rational response. The system as it is doesn't serve the police and it clearly doesn't serve the public.

The culture creates an internal hostile environment that police officers become immersed in. A manifestation of this environment is the predominance of officers with dismal personal lives plagued by divorce and broken homes. The great misnomer is that a police career is a stressful job because of the dangers they encounter. The truth is that the stress is an internal problem. Police stress is created by the police culture itself. Police departments create unspoken codes that are used inside the police realm to justify conduct that is exercised on the general public. The problem is the general public isn't attuned to and does not adhere to the unwritten rules and double standards that are rooted deep within the police culture. When faced with the most blatant misconduct the police command staff become more defiant, staunchly sticking to their old rhetoric.

It is important to note that the majority of police shootings are completely justifiable given the circumstances that officers face and these incidents legitimize the real dangers encountered by police officers. However, the existence of this real danger cannot be an excuse to nullify the misconduct of others.

Hopefully this book can give the reader an inside look at how dysfunctional the inner police world is. This book will illustrate the aberrations entrenched in the police culture. The police have drifted drastically away from what should be their core principles of truth and justice. The system as it is has reached the point where men who are void of any character or ability, rise to the highest levels of power. It allows the corrupt to rise while the honest are crushed. With this glimpse into the police mentality, one can then try to understand more clearly how we have reached this point of justifiable distrust of law enforcement.

The Kennedy Incident

The calls started coming in over the radio while I sat in my cruiser in the precinct parking lot at the other end of the city, watching the windshield wipers whip back and forth in an attempt to fight back the torrent of rain coming down from the sky. It had been an unusually slow night, likely due to the rain, and the shift was almost over.

Car-1 with Richie Leavitt had been dispatched to check out a suspicious vehicle parked near the end of Bennington Terrace, a dead-end street in the quietest sector in the city. Nobody gave it much thought until the next call came in.

"We're getting calls of an armed home invasion in progress on Varnum Ave."

"Car-11, start heading over to Car-1's location, in case that vehicle is somehow related."

The Varnum Avenue address was right around the corner from Bennington Terrace, so there was a chance that it was.

"Right, I'm heading that way right now," Donny Crawford responded.

I assumed the situation was handled and began to prepare for the end of my shift.

"We've got guys at gunpoint, we've got two guys at gunpoint! There's guys running! Start sending cars!" Crawford's call for help cracked frantically over the radio. Dispatch immediately sent several cars, including me, to assist.

I started driving that way from the Lower Highlands, on the opposite side of the city. I knew it would take me a little while to get there, and I figured the whole thing would be over by the time I drove across town to provide assistance. Sure enough, I was one of the last officers at the scene, but the situation was far from over when I arrived. Nine cruisers arrived before me and I had to park some distance away from the action.

I scanned the scene as I walked toward Bennington Terrace from my car. "Where the hell is everybody?" I thought as I got closer and only saw a couple of guys.

Leavitt's cruiser blocked what we now know to be the getaway car for the home invasion, and two of the suspects sat in the back seat of the car. Crawford and Leavitt stood with their guns drawn, tension flickering through the air as they aimed their weapons at the getaway car. Sergeant Buckley stood right next to the suspect vehicle, completely lit up by the take down lights from the cruiser. As I arrived, he threw his hands up in the air and spun around in circles like a top while making hooting sounds. You can't make this shit up. Before I could figure out what he was doing, he ran past me into the darkness towards Varnum Avenue.

"He's in charge here, why is he running away?" I thought briefly before turning my attention back to the scene at hand. I knew Buckley to be a suck ass and an idiot, so his behavior, while dangerously odd and out of line, didn't surprise me too much.

I later found out that Buckley sent all the units into the woods to look for the fleeing suspects, leaving no one to help Leavitt and Crawford with the suspects in the vehicle.

"Seems the immediate threat isn't an issue for Buckley," I thought as I turned to Crawford.

"Hey Donny, what have you got?"

"I think these guys are armed," he replied, barely taking his eyes off the car to acknowledge me.

"Okay, let's set up a felony car stop. Do you want me to run it?"

"Ok Bob, ya," he nodded, visibly relieved that he finally had some help.

The stop belonged to Crawford and Leavitt, and etiquette-wise, running the call was their responsibility. However, it was clear to me they were unsure what the next step should be and they needed a little assistance to get them going. Realistically, a supervisor should have taken over at that point, but he had just been spinning around like a crazy person before he ran off into the night. I was a team leader on the NEMLEC (North East Massachusetts Law Enforcement Council) SWAT team and an instructor in the Lowell, Massachusetts, police department. I taught the felony car stop procedure for SWAT, and I had experience with the procedure on the street, so I felt very comfortable with assisting.

While I spoke to Crawford, Jack Davis arrived and took up a position next to Leavitt. Jack was the chief's brother, and at 6'7" and 400 pounds, he wasn't going to be running in the woods chasing suspects. I acknowledged him as part of our takedown team at the getaway car as I took over the commands and began to get the suspects and the scene under control.

"You in the vehicle! Put your hands up on the roof."

Neither suspect moved.

"I know you speak English. Now put your hands on the roof! Do it!"

Their hands slowly came up.

"Now keep them there." I waited just a moment to ensure they were complying before continuing.

"Left side passenger, open the door and keep your hands where I can see them. That's right keep 'em up."

The suspects responded to my commands without any issues and the operation was running smoothly. Once I had the first suspect lying face down on the ground, I felt the situation was manageable. I handed the commands back over to Crawford because it was his felony car stop.

I stepped back to the cruisers to turn off some of the lights so the officers would not be such a target. Leavitt and Crawford turned their takedown and alley lights on when they arrived at the scene, not realizing what exactly they were getting into, and we were lit up more than the suspects. We needed to lose some lighting to give us more concealment.

As I turned off the lights, Officer Tommy Kennedy arrived on the scene. Kennedy was a rookie; he only had about three years on the job, and he was one of those entitled kids who thinks they can have anything they want. His father was the city auditor, and he had no problems making sure everyone knew it. In the police world there is a cultural hierarchy that is very similar to the medieval feudal system of royalty and peasant. Kennedy was royalty and I would learn very quickly I was a peasant.

"Get out of the car, lay on the ground, and put your hands out to your sides," Crawford instructed the second suspect to do what the first suspect had just finished doing.

Suddenly, Kennedy interrupted, shouting over Crawford.

"Hey asshole, don't fucking move, don't fucking move!"

Everyone turned toward Kennedy, shocked and confused, even the suspects. Not only did his orders completely contradict the direct order that Crawford had just given, they also contradicted the tone and consistency of the entire felony car stop that we had conducted before Kennedy's arrival. No one seemed to know what to do next.

"Only one man gives the commands!" I ordered from my position behind the cruiser, and Kennedy backed down.

Soon, both suspects were on the ground with their hands out to their sides. Crawford and I moved forward to place them in handcuffs. While we dealt with the suspects, Jack Davis performed a visual scan of the area and found a sawed off shotgun in the mud on the ground next to the passenger door, confirming our suspicion that the suspects were armed. We called for a wagon to come pick up the suspects and Crawford and Leavitt remained to guard them until it arrived.

I heard Buckley on the radio, calling for the fire department to bring lights to Varnum Avenue. I couldn't figure out why they needed lights, but with the suspects handcuffed and the scene secure, I wasn't needed anymore. I decided to head over toward Varnum Avenue and see if I could assist with finding the other two suspects.

On the way there, I noticed Kennedy standing by Leavitt's car with his gun drawn. I approached him.

"Have you ever done a felony car stop before?"

I wasn't mad, I'd been on plenty of scenes that had gotten screwed up, and mistakes happened, but I did feel he should have known better. You don't show up on someone else's scene and just start screaming, especially when the officers are dealing with armed suspects.

"Yeah," he sniffed arrogantly, puffing himself up.

"Only one man gives the commands," I repeated what I told him before in a disgusted tone and I walked away. I had pandered to his arrogance too much in the past to want to deal with it tonight. I only managed to make it a few steps before I heard him behind me, shouting.

"Hey, who the fuck do you think you are?" I kept walking and he started to pursue me, still screaming.

"Who the fuck do you think you are! Turn around!"

I kept walking.

"Turn the fuck around!" he shouted petulantly.

I continued walking away for about a hundred feet with him on my heels shouting at my back. Finally, I turned around. Here was this five foot nothing pudgy kid standing in front of me, visibly fighting off tears. His lower lip quivered, and his eyes welled up.

"Get away from me," I stated, hoping he would do the right thing and step back. He obviously needed to compose himself. He didn't really seem to know what to do now with me facing him, and he stood there confused for a moment before he punched me in the chest.

"What a joke," I thought. Kennedy had more energy invested into holding back tears than he did into his punch. On top of that, I wore a ballistic vest with a plate, and he didn't have much strength to begin with. I placed my open hand on his chest and pushed him away with my fingers, shocked to see this kid falling apart in front of me.

Kennedy responded by punching me in the jaw, a punch as pathetic and ridiculous as the first.

"Do not hit him," I thought as I grabbed him by the shoulder and spun him around to hold him in a bear hug. I held him down like a child having a tantrum as I held my face close to his ear.

"Calm down," I said. "Calm down, Tommy, calm down." I repeated myself, hoping the message would get through.

Buckley came running over to us from where he had been on Varnum Avenue.

"Break it up!" he shouted.

When Kennedy heard Buckley's voice he stopped struggling. I let him go and stepped away. Buckley arrived and used both of his hands to push me further from Kennedy as I backed up.

"I don't know what happened here, but I want reports from both of you," Buckley said, looking us both over. I pulled him to the side.

"Look, the kid screwed up. Let's just leave it at that. I don't want to get him into any trouble."

"Write it anyway," Buckley replied. "Nothing's going to happen."

"That's probably true," I thought to myself as I walked off. "With his connections, he probably won't get into any trouble at all."

The next day, Buckley and I met up in a parking lot during our shift to talk about the events of the previous evening.

"Kennedy called me at home last night to tell me what happened," he began. "You shouldn't have spoken to him like that, you should have known it would upset him." Kennedy's family was close to Buckley's family, and their brothers were good friends.

"Did you talk to any of the other guys who were there?"

"No, I don't have to," Buckley replied tersely.

"Look Mark, I've instructed him in the past during motorcycle school and firearms instruction. I wasn't speaking to him any differently than I would have during class. I just told him that only one man should give the commands. That's procedure and we do it that way to keep everyone safe."

"Well, you embarrassed him," Buckley responded.

"He embarrassed himself."

"You shouldn't have spoken to him like that. Nothing's going to happen with this anyway, but you need to watch what you say to guys when you're out on patrol from now on."

I left, a little bewildered, thinking I had heard the last of it.

The following day, I worked my sector on the motorcycle with my partner, Mark Bruso. It was a very standard night, and we stopped to get dinner around eight. While there, I got a call from my shift commander.

"Where are you? I need to talk to you."

He came to the restaurant where Bruso and I were eating and I stepped outside to talk.

"Look, don't shoot the messenger," he said. "Okay?"

I looked at him warily as I nodded.

"Buckley just spoke with Ed Davis about that Kennedy thing the other night. Davis wants you suspended. He also wants you off of SWAT and he is removing you from all of your instructor positions as of right now. I was told to tell you to turn in your SWAT weapons immediately."

He had a pained expression on his face as he continued. "Also, he wants you off the motorcycle, too. You're to bring it in now and park it before you get all your gear."

"What?" I asked, completely shocked. "What the hell is going on? Is there an investigation, is internal affairs interviewing anyone?"

"No, I don't think so. Davis is dealing with this himself."

"It hasn't even been forty-eight hours. Has anyone other than Buckley and Davis even had time to review this?" I couldn't understand why I was losing all my positions over what happened, when I had done nothing wrong.

"Look," he said. "All I know is the Chief just heard about it, and this is how he is handling it. I'm just relaying the orders. You need to return the bike now and go home to get all your gear." He looked down at the ground for a second and then looked back at me. "Sorry Bob."

I left the restaurant and turned in my bike, and then went home to get all my gear, thinking that my name would be cleared as soon as they investigated further. I thought I handled it better than most guys would have reacted to getting punched in the face, and I was confident that at some point the truth would come out and I could quickly put this whole thing behind me.

I didn't realize it then, but the decision to suspend me was entirely based on what Kennedy told Buckley on the night of the incident, when Kennedy called him at home after our shift ended. They only had three reports regarding the incident when I was notified in writing that I would be suspended. My report, which was an "assault and battery on a police officer" report with Kennedy listed as the suspect (Alvarez 1, 3). They had Kennedy's report, which stated he followed me as I walked away. He reported I turned around and that he grabbed me by the collar and pushed me away (Kennedy T., 2), but nowhere in Kennedy's report does it say I hit or struck him.

They also had Buckley's initial report, which said he heard me yell that only one officer should give the orders. Buckley continues with "this was the right way to conduct the stop and the officers realized this" (Buckley, 13 Apr., 1997). Buckley said he was 30 to 40 feet away when he heard a commotion and saw me approach Kennedy and yell at him. He then wrote that we got into a mutual scuffle and he had to physically get between the two of us. This was the information that they had on file when I received written notification of my suspension. The problem with all of this was that Buckley was not 30 to 40 feet away, he was on an entirely different street and he could not see what was going on between myself and Kennedy.

After my suspension, the other officers present that evening turned in their reports. Every other report that came in about the events of that evening stated that, due to the rain (Crawford, 2), the lights (Davis, 2), and a set of eight foot tall shrubs (Leavitt, 2), they could not see what happened between Kennedy and myself. They were all standing right there and they all saw what Kennedy did, but they chose to omit it from their reports. Regardless, the reports did not support Buckley's version of the events.

Buckley actually wrote two conflicting reports about the events of the evening; one that said he saw everything (Buckley, 13 Apr., 1997), and one that said he was about 30 to 40 feet away when he heard a commotion coming from where we were (Buckley, 18 Apr., 1997). All of this was unknown by Davis when his decision to suspend me was made, and subsequently ignored by him in his refusal to rescind my suspension.

This was my first experience with receiving a disciplinary action in ten years as a police officer. I had nothing negative in my personnel file, only awards and letters of thanks for professional performance. In all that time, I had never heard of anyone receiving such a harsh punishment for similar behavior. I wasn't guilty of what I had been accused of doing, and I knew that I hadn't done anything wrong, so I refused to accept the punishment that had been meted out to me. I appealed the decision, not knowing that I had started a fight that would become a fourteen-year-long battle.

After I filed my appeal, Chief Davis held a command staff meeting where he apparently instructed his command staff to find any way they possibly could to discipline or suspend me. After the meeting, Captain Bobbie Demoura grabbed one of my direct commanders, Sergeant Laferriere, to tell him that Davis wanted him to keep an eye on me to see if they could screw me on anything. Laferriere was a decent guy and gave me the heads up.

"They know you didn't do anything wrong, but they aren't going to drop it. It looks like he is out to get you, Bob. Be careful."

I didn't fully understand the seriousness of his warning yet, or how the fact that Davis was now out to get me would lead to the demise of my career and any progress that I had made toward my goals for the future at that point. It's hard to recall what I was feeling at this time. None of it made sense to me; it felt a little bit like a dream, but the situation was all too real. I was totally awestruck and in shock. How was I supposed to respond to this? What actions could I take to straighten this out? Was there a way to recover my career? How long will this situation last? Months? Years? Forever?

I would later come to learn that I wasn't the first person to whom Davis had done this. His career is littered with the lives of men and women who he chose to go after and harm. Davis earned respect through fear, and I was to become just one of his many victims.

NEMLEC Chief's Meetings

Shortly after the Kennedy incident, the chiefs of the area police departments that were a part of NEMLEC met to discuss the possible restructuring of the SWAT team. Ed Davis called for the meetings because he claimed to be concerned about the actions of the team during the funeral of one of our members who had died. Frank Roarke, who was the commander of SWAT, attended the meetings to answer to all of the accusations that Davis was making against the team.

Davis wanted to change the way NEMLEC appointed officers to SWAT. He felt the appointments should rotate, in order to give all officers in all departments the opportunity to be on the team if they so wanted. Davis hoped to drop all the qualifications and set it up so anyone who aspired to be on SWAT would get to serve on the team for a year.

Roarke strongly advised against this and demonstrated to the other chiefs that dropping the qualifications and not valuing the experience of SWAT personnel would be a disaster. SWAT operations are sometimes fraught with danger and high levels of stress. Officers need to build experience, and it takes well more than one year to be able to respond to changes in the situation at hand properly. Officers on SWAT must be able to maintain their cool, and not react negatively if things go wrong. This is why it is extremely important that the team members receive a higher level of training by experienced instructors before joining the team on operations, and why the requirements for joining the team were so stringent. In order to emphasize that experience was the key to success, Roarke went on to share the details of a specific SWAT team operation that could have had a completely different outcome had it not been for the advanced skill level of the team members.

The team had a search warrant for Dominicans dealing drugs from an apartment in Lowell. We scheduled the raid for late at night, hoping to catch the drug dealers by surprise. It was a third-floor apartment, and we planned to enter through the kitchen. We were moving very quickly and quietly because operations like this require us to get in and get the suspects before they have a chance to react and dispose of evidence.

We entered the kitchen that night and I immediately knew something wasn't right. I have been in a number of drug houses, and the apartment we were in did not match my expectations at all. The kitchen was clean, with a high chair and children's drawings posted on the refrigerator. I quickly recognized that we were not in the right apartment.

"All stop! Alpha Team, all stop!" I called off on the radio to the team.

It was the right call and all the other guys on entry team had enough experience to realize we were in the wrong place too. In that split second when we breached the door we all got the sense something was wrong and my radio call was the reinforcement needed to backup what we were all feeling. Everyone immediately responded to my call and stood fast.

We later discovered we had been given the wrong address. The apartment we entered was occupied by a family with small children and an elderly grandmother, and if we didn't stop at the threshold the family probably would have sued. It was a decision made in half a heartbeat and it saved the department from a deep-pocket lawsuit, and potentially saved the family from harm as well.

Before this incident, the SWAT team in Boston had also been given the wrong address for a search warrant. During this operation, no one on that team recognized the fact that they were in the wrong house, and an innocent man was killed (Unknown, 1994). The Boston Police force had to deal with a lot of negative publicity and it also had to pay a large settlement to the man's family. Unfortunately, incidents where SWAT teams receive bad information and enter the wrong house happen (Brodey). It is essential that the officers be highly experienced in order quickly to recognize when they might be in the wrong home to protect innocent civilians.

There are lots of other examples where having an experienced officer is vital to SWAT team operations. Experience is highly valued in many careers for good reason, and in organizations like SWAT it is necessary for a person to achieve expert, not novice, skill level. SWAT ops can be life-and-death missions and the wrong decision can leave officers and civilians dead. Not all operations are life and death and I want to stress that the reality of SWAT is actually much different from what the public imagines it to be. However, it is still extremely important that the guys on the team have the necessary experience and skill set for when things do go wrong. This experience and skill cannot be gained in only a year. Based on his recommendations for the team, Ed Davis didn't understand this.

There are a lot of cops who constantly go to training schools, and on paper they may appear to have all the necessary skills. But often, these guys never really work the street and they have no real experience. The requirements for SWAT included operational experience for a reason: it was a requirement designed to save lives. Ed

Davis' plan to have rotating positions would not have satisfied this requirement. Luckily, Lieutenant Roarke managed to effectively communicate this to the other chiefs and they did not choose to implement Davis' plan.

Unfortunately, Roarke could not give me credit for being the team leader that had realized this mistake and ordered the team to halt, and he omitted my name when he told the story. Davis had been telling the chiefs who were present at the meeting that I was "a danger to other police officers" and that I was a "militant rogue" with a bad attitude. He did such a good job convincing them about my mental instability that Roarke feared the effect he needed the story to have would be lost if they knew that the experienced officer he was talking about was me. As my direct supervisor, Roarke knew these things were not true, but the other chiefs had never had a chance to work with me directly and were influenced by Davis' accusations.

In fact, Roarke and I worked on many operations together and he knew I made sound decisions under pressure. Even though some incidents did reach the level where deadly force would have been justified, I was consistently able to use a lower level of force to subdue suspects. One of these operations was actually one of the SWAT team's first barricaded gunman incidents in 1988. We were called to North Andover where officers responded to call in an apartment complex for a man with a gun. They located the man pictured, and when they arrived, he threatened to shoot the officers before retreating into the house.

"Someone is going to die! Someone is going to die!" he yelled repeatedly. The officers called in SWAT, and we responded and set up a perimeter. While negotiators attempted to contact him by phone, he suddenly appeared at the front door directly in front of me with a handgun.

"Well what are you going to do? Are you going to shoot or am I?" he yelled at me in an excited voice.

"Come on John, just put the gun down," I responded. I knew his first name but that was about it. I didn't know his history or his situation.

He held the pistol with one hand and waved it in my direction. I knew the only real target he had was my face and neck because I had the cover from behind the parked car and I was wearing a ballistic tactical vest and ballistic helmet. I also knew, based on my own shooting ability, that he would have a difficult time making that shot with one hand and would need a few seconds to steady his hand and get a good sight picture to be able to do so. I felt confident he couldn't achieve that level of accuracy, but I couldn't give him the benefit of the doubt, so I clicked the safety off my SPAS-12 and settled into a good shooting posture.

I watched the pistol in his hand intently, knowing that I would take the shot if I saw the full muzzle of the gun pointed at me. I was loaded with double O buck which would pretty much tear him up at such a close range. I kept calling him by name to put the gun down and just end the whole thing. As we continued our dialogue, other officers started to appear in our periphery, which seemed to overwhelm him. He turned and ran back into the house. After that, he wouldn't answer the phone and all communication stopped.

Ultimately, we deployed gas into the house which forced him out, and he was taken into custody alive and unharmed. This incident demonstrated to the NEMLEC chiefs that their fears that the SWAT team would be trigger happy were misplaced. The team continued on to build a professional reputation over the next few years.

In 1989, I had only been a member of the SWAT Team a year or so when the FBI contacted the team because an incarcerated informant had told them that his old gang from Chelsea was planning to hit a high-end jewelry store in the town of Westford, a quiet and affluent suburban town northwest of Boston. At the time there were only two jewelry stores in Westford, and we took an educated guess that the one that was in the center of town in a plaza was the target. We started staking out the jewelry store in the evenings because our intelligence indicated the store would be targeted at nine p.m., closing time.

We set up in the Plaza with two undercover SWAT vans; one carried the assault team and the other carried the surveillance team that videotaped the front of the jewelry store. We also had three SWAT members stationed in the back room of the store. Westford Police were stationed in secluded areas outside the perimeter in marked patrol units and unmarked cars. They were instructed to respond only if they received a radio call from the SWAT commander, Lieutenant Roarke.

I was positioned in the rear of the assault team van with George Thistle from the Wakefield Police Department. The two of us were to exit through the van's rear doors. Four other guys were seated in the middle of the van to exit through the right-side sliding door. Lieutenant Roarke was in charge of the operation overall. He was in plain clothes in the driver's seat and was responsible for radio communications.

The first few nights were uneventful. We just sat there in full gear for a couple of hours shooting the breeze until the store closed. Most of the guys carried 9mm MP-5's and AR rifles, but I had just started carrying the SPAS-12 Auto shotgun. There was a Market Basket supermarket next door that was considerably busy those evenings. I had chosen to load double O buck, and I remember thinking that I really needed to beware of pedestrians down range in the parking lot if this turned into an actual incident.

On the fourth night, it had been quiet as usual and we were just about ready to go home when nine o'clock rolled around. Suddenly the radio cracked with Dave Seamans from the surveillance van.

"It's going down! It's going down!" he yelled.

Roarke slammed the van into drive and punched it hard as he pulled out of the parking space. He yelled back to us several short and excited sentences as he maneuvered the van into place.

"Brown sedan pulled up in front!"

"There's suspects running into the store!"

"I'm putting the van in front of the suspect vehicle!"

"Hold on!"

Everything that happened next all transpired over a 15-to-20-second time span.

Roarke drove wildly through the parking lot and slammed on the brakes right in front of the suspect vehicle. When he did this, we all were thrown forward violently and the van side door was flung forward, slamming shut and jamming. The middle guys were trapped inside. George and I bailed out the rear doors and moved to the sidewalk.

As we screeched to a halt one of the robbers ran out of the store. He jumped over the hood of his car and got behind the wheel. Since part of the team was trapped in the van, Roarke had to react, so he jumped out from the driver's seat and drew down on the suspect with a mini-14. The suspect punched it and drove up onto the sidewalk, trying to hit Roarke. as he quickly fired a round and jumped out of the way.

I heard the shot and heard the car coming, and I looked to see that it was now barreling down the sidewalk. As George stepped onto the curb, the car's left headlight and fender slammed into his legs. I was right behind him with the SPAS-12 muzzle up. As the car hit him, I grabbed him by the back of his ballistic vest and pulled him back, saving him from falling in front of the car and getting run over. George's body slid down the outside of the car as it sped by, down the front fender to the driver's door.

At one point the robber was only two feet away from us through the window glass. He had a baseball hat on backwards and his eyes and mouth were completely wide open. As the car passed, I let George go and immediately dropped the muzzle of my shotgun down. It came to rest high on my forearm and I pulled the trigger. The nine 32cal pellets of my double O round impacted the quarter panel in a three-foot pattern and the car swerved violently to the left. I realized that he was trying to get to the parking lot exit on the left, and the car was almost broadside to me now.

Now I had both hands on my weapon and got in a good shooting position. I pulled the trigger and the whole driver's door window glass exploded and collapsed in on the driver. The car swerved to the right as it was heading out of the parking lot. I knew I had hit him and thought to myself that he was done. As the car was heading out of the parking lot, David Seamans got out of the surveillance van and lit up the car with his MP-5, taking out a couple of tires.

Almost at the same time, gunfire erupted from inside the jewelry store. As the robbers entered, the first robber, who carried a sawed off automatic shotgun, ran through smashing jewelry cases. The other robber followed him, reaching in and filling bags. When they saw their ride leave and heard the gunfire, they ran to the back of the store where the inside team was waiting. Bob Marchionda, a close friend of mine who was also on the team, later told me that when he looked out the door, he was surprised to see the robber with the shotgun right in front of him. He fired a round of double O from the hip but it missed and hit the counter. This was about when I entered the store myself.

Mackenzie was behind Marchionda with an M-16 and fired two rounds. The first bullet hit the robber's shotgun right on the bolt at the chamber, jamming the gun. The second bullet hit him high in the chest and exited out his shoulder. The other robber was unarmed and just hit the ground. He put his hands on his head in total fear.

Roarke and I swept the front of the shop, and checked that the two women clerks who cowered behind the counter were okay. The robber who we shot was laying on the floor whimpering and pleading for an ambulance. Roarke kicked the shotgun away and then kicked the robber in the chest.

"Shut the fuck up!" When Roarke kicked him, it made blood squirt out of his shoulder where he was shot.

Now that the scene was secure, I left to check on the robber in the car outside. Westford patrol units came on the scene as I stepped outside.

"We never got the call that the robbery was going down," they said. "What the hell happened?" they asked, confused.

It took me a second to realize what had happened. When the guys got trapped in the van, Roarke had to react quickly and take action. He stepped out of his role of running communication, and never advised the other units of the situation. As we were discussing the debacle, another unit called in. They had located the getaway car, abandoned across the street behind a building with the engine running. I immediately headed over there.

When I arrived, I saw that the two rear tires had been shot out and were flat. The driver's door was open and the baseball hat the robber wore was on the ground by the door. It had three bullet holes in it, but there was no blood. There was no blood in the car or on the ground. As I was looking around, Dave Seamans stepped over.

"That cat had some kind of fuck'n angel on his shoulder," he said as he looked at the hat.

These robbers were good, the shot up getaway car had just been reported stolen a half hour earlier. They used that car to commit the robbery and had a second car laid off to flee the area in. That car was stationed behind the building across the street where we found the getaway car shot up. It made no difference, because all three of the suspects were identified before the whole thing went down. The guy who got away was arrested a few months later in New Jersey. He reported that he had been hit in the left side when pellet fragments went through the door, but it was minor and it healed with no problem. Other than that, he came through the whole thing unscathed. This was the first and last time the SWAT team ever fired its weapons in an operation up to the date of this writing, in 2016.

After Davis removed me from the SWAT team, Timmy Crowley was left as the only member on the team from Lowell. Davis highly favored Crowley, and it became clear that he put a lot of pressure on Roarke to have Crowley fall into the role that was now open due to my removal. He miraculously became a team leader and started doing firearms qualifications shortly afterward, even though he only had a minimal amount of skill or experience. Could this be part of the reason why Davis pushed so hard to get me off the team?

Roarke's wife later revealed that her husband struggled to maintain control over the team with Crowley as a team leader because they had no respect for him. At one point, Roarke had to order the team to stop making fun of Crowley behind his back because it hurt team morale. They started "false praising" him instead, saying things such as, "Wow, what a great job!" in an over-exaggerated tone. They had reasons for their lack of respect. Although Crowley didn't cry at the drop of hat like Kennedy, what I saw of his SWAT performance was pathetic in my opinion. He rarely showed up to SWAT call outs, and often missed training days, so we couldn't really judge his abilities based on those activities. His performance at SWAT Round Up, however, was a completely different story.

All through the nineties, Roarke had the team compete at the SWAT Round Up in Orlando, Florida, an international competition of approximately 70 to 80 SWAT teams. The teams are mostly from the United States, but it qualifies as an international competition because some overseas teams, like Germany's elite GSG9, participate. The teams come to compete in a number of events: the three-gun shoot, tower scramble, Prencher scramble, officer rescue, and an obstacle course event. The competition at Round Up is pretty stiff.

Approximately fifteen of the teams are full time SWAT teams, and they usually command the first fifteen finals places. The other 60 or so teams are part-time teams like NEMLEC.

Of the six competitions that NEMLEC attended, Crowley only competed twice. The first time was in 1991 when he made a firearms safety violation. This got the team disqualified for that event and led to the NEMLEC team coming in at last place out of 75 teams.

Crowley competed again in 1996. The year before, I operated as the team leader for the competition team, and we finished in a respectable 26th place. This was the best we had ever done, and we had high hopes of doing even better the following year. Then one of our guys had to drop out, and Roarke chose Crowley to replace him. Crowley and I were the designated handgun shooters for the first event, a hostage rescue scenario called the three-gun shoot. We were to enter a house and shoot ten steel targets, each ranging anywhere from five to ten yards away.

I entered the house, shot my ten rounds, and ran out. I picked up the hostage dummy and waited for Crowley to catch up, but he didn't come. He hit three of the ten targets, and kept shooting at the rest and missing. He was burning up seconds on the clock and running out of ammo.

"Bob! Take his place!" Roarke yelled from the sidelines.

I dropped the dummy and ran in, tapping Crowley.

"Switch!"

I quickly dropped his last seven targets and ran up right behind him as he headed for the door. Our time was awful, but I hoped we might be able to somehow catch up in the other events. I was wrong. In the next two shooting events, Crowley again made two major firearms safety violations and the team was disqualified (DQ'ed) again. DQ'ed means you're put in last place, with zero points. To make things even more embarrassing, Crowley cried foul, accusing the range safety officer of being wrong and taking his complaint to the competition judges. The judges pointed out that the line safety officers are unbiased referees and their observations don't change whether he liked it or not. Crowley had become accustomed to being in Lowell where he always got his way, but that doesn't work in the rest of the world.

Ultimately, we came in second to last place, 75th place out of 76 teams. Crowley's performance clearly demonstrated he was one of the worst SWAT cops in the United States. If you fall apart in competition and can't handle that stress, how would anyone expect you to perform in real operations? At least he didn't cry.

This was the guy with whom Davis wanted to replace me, the guy who did replace me, and the guy who started teaching firearms to the men on the team after I left. Thankfully, during the time Crowley was a team leader, there were no major incidents or operations that required real leadership. I believe he was able to coast through with his position until he ultimately quit, which was probably the safest way to maintain his image before his incompetence came to light. Due to his close ties with Davis, Crowley's poor performance never came into question and he continued to receive promotions and accolades while working in Lowell.

Davis didn't just publicly slander me at the NEMLEC chief's meetings. He also tried to get Roarke, my friend and commander on SWAT, to turn against me as well. According to what Roarke told me, Davis couldn't understand why I held a leadership position or how I earned the respect of my team members. Why are all these guys following the lead of someone like Alvarez? Someone like me who was a minority.

At one of the NEMLEC chief's meetings, Roarke was questioned about how I spent my personal vacations, with Davis asking him if he knew of my involvement in a "secret society" and "The Occult." Roarke was specifically asked if he knew anything about how I "secretly would go into the woods and build shrines." Apparently this was how the chiefs interpreted my mountain climbing trips in the White Mountains of New Hampshire.

When Roarke later told me about all of this, I was flabbergasted. The job had always been dominated by the Irish, like Kennedy and Crowley, and it just wasn't right in Davis' mind that a minority outperformed white guys. There must be another answer. It was hinted at that instead of my skill and ability being the reason, that I must have them under some sort of spell or curse. These NEMLEC chiefs meetings consisted of police chiefs from approximately 30 cities and towns north of Boston, who were responsible for providing leadership in law enforcement and the protection of over a million American citizens. If what Roarke told me was the truth, then that means they found it acceptable that their main topic of discussion at these meetings was over rumors about my vacation time, if I had tattoos, and if I secretly built shrines in the woods.

Once I really started to understand that my career wasn't going to go anywhere in Lowell under the leadership of Ed Davis, I attempted to transfer back to Waltham, where I had been prior to moving to Lowell. I earned respect while working as an officer there, and I believed it would be better if I moved back.

When I was originally hired on in Waltham, I was called to Chief Unsworth's office on my first day for a welcome-to-the-department meeting. During our conversation, the chief said he spoke with the psychologist who did my psychological screening. He said in all his years as chief he had never received a profile where the psychologist concluded that an officer would be best in a leadership role rather than just as a patrolman. I had no reason to suspect that my request for transfer would be problematic. Unfortunately, I had no concept of the power that Davis held over the other chiefs in the area. After my request was denied, I spoke to Captain Drew in Waltham and he informed me that Chief Unsworth wouldn't allow the transfer because he didn't want to get involved and cross Davis. Nobody ever wanted to cross Davis.

I later found out that Tommy Kennedy applied for a position in the Nashua New Hampshire Police Department prior to Lowell. I heard that he failed the psychological screening and he was not hired. Kennedy didn't take a psychological screening in Lowell because it wasn't required. If Lowell had conducted a background check before hiring Kennedy, they would have seen that Nashua refused to hire him because of this. This should have prevented Kennedy from getting hired in Lowell as well. Either they didn't check, or they did and they ignored it.

City Manager and Civil Service Hearing

The first step in the process of my appeal was a hearing before the city manager. I used an attorney, Richard Sullivan, provided by the patrolmen's union to represent my case. He appeared to be capable and to be on my side, at least at first. Sullivan advised me that the city manager for Lowell, Brian Martin, was in cahoots with Davis and would just "rubber stamp" the case. We didn't even bother with putting a serious defense together because we knew it was pointless.

For the hearing, we all sat around a table in a conference room. There were no witnesses; it was just Deputy Chief Dennis Cormier, Buckley, Martin, and myself. Cormier and Buckley explained their reasoning to Martin for the decision to suspend me. I defended myself by repeating, "there is no evidence to support what you are saying," every time they accused me of something, on the advice of my lawyer.

Buckley lied and said he had done "hundreds" of felony car stops, which wouldn't have even been possible over the length of his career. As a reference for comparison, I only did a little over a dozen felony car stops over my entire career. If there was some forewarning that an incident might require a felony stop, I was requested to respond and provide assistance, even if it was out of my sector.

Then they claimed that it wasn't my place to speak to Kennedy at all because the scene wasn't secured, yet Buckley stated that my actions were appropriate in his initial report. Buckley would later testify in court that the scene was secure.

By the time everything was over, I was a little shocked. I knew Buckley was going to blame me when we went into the hearing because his attitude was that it was my fault from the beginning, but I never expected him to lie as extensively as he did.

At this point, Buckley's main argument was that my behavior was inappropriate because there were civilians present and it was an active crime scene. This was in spite of the fact that, again, his initial report stated the opposite. Later the story would evolve into him testifying that I hit Kennedy.

The finding from the city manager's hearing came back a week later. It said that they found my conduct outrageous and inappropriate and the decision to suspend me was upheld. This did not surprise me because my lawyer told me to expect it.

We appealed the decision again and took it to the next level, as a civil service hearing. Before the civil service trial, Sullivan prepared me for what to expect.

"I just want to tell you ahead of time that the commission usually finds in favor of the chiefs of police, so don't be surprised if you lose. Most likely we'll have to appeal the case to a superior court judge."

I nodded, beginning to wonder how far I was really going to have to end up taking this thing.

The civil service hearing was more formal than the city hearing and actually took place in a hearing room. Buckley committed perjury again by lying on the stand.

"I was on Varnum Ave. and the felony car stop was on Bennington Terrace."

"So you felt it was more important to be on Varnum Ave. than to be at the felony car stop?" my lawyer asked.

"As I already stated I was only 20 feet away."

"Were you supervising the felony motor vehicle stop?"

"Yes."

"Did you review any of the other officers' reports before filing your second report?"

"I don't recall," Buckley shifted in his seat.

"In your reports there is no reference to Officer Alvarez striking Officer Kennedy, is there?"

"No."

"Does your report say that Officer Kennedy took a swing at Officer Alvarez?"

"Yes."

"So you saw Officer Kennedy take a swing at Officer Alvarez?"

"Yes sir."

"You said specifically that Officer Kennedy swung on Officer Alvarez. What I'm asking you is did you see Officer Alvarez take a swing at Officer Kennedy?"

"They got physical."

"So you saw Officer Alvarez take a swing at Officer Kennedy?"

"They were both swinging. Yes sir."

"But you didn't find a need to put that in your report?"

"No. My feeling at the time it was mutual thing. I didn't see any particular strikes."

"So you didn't see any striking?"

"Both arms were going. I didn't see… I didn't see."

"It's a simple question Sergeant. Did you see Officer Alvarez strike Officer Kennedy?"

"As far as I'm concerned. Yes, as far as I'm concerned."

"But you didn't feel it necessary to put that in your report?"

"No, I did not."

If Buckley was 20 feet away he would have been standing at the rear bumper of Leavitt's cruiser, which he was not. His reports said he was 30 to 40 feet away, but he was actually on Varnum Street.

When Kennedy got on the stand, he asked for permission to just read from his report and not answer questions directly.

"Your report has already been introduced into evidence," my attorney replied aggressively. "No."

This was the first time Kennedy had testified in court, and he was nervous. He had been a cop for three years and never once testified as a police officer. His first time would be against another cop, me ... a cop he knew was innocent. When questioned, Kennedy stated he was well versed with the felony car stop, and testified that he had done ten felony car stops in the past. It was later learned he had done none.

"He started screaming at me," Kennedy stated. "He walked away with his back to me, screaming. I wanted to have a civil conversation but he kept screaming. I did grab him by the collar."

After stating this, Kennedy testified that I did not strike him and he did not strike me.

This testimony conflicted with what Buckley just said on the stand, and it also conflicted with what I would say. When I was on the stand, my testimony was completely different than Buckley's.

"Why is it that you seem to remember the events of that evening so differently from Sergeant Buckley?" the city attorney asked.

"He wasn't there," I responded. "He didn't see what happened."

"Oh, so Sergeant Buckley is lying?"

"Yes."

The room fell silent. It took a moment for the attorney to compose himself again before continuing with his line of questioning. Originally I thought this was a good thing, but the silence occurred because I had actually just broken an unspoken rule. You never call another cop above you in rank a liar, especially if you're a minority. The general belief is cops don't lie and if a minority accuses a white cop of lying, then he's just playing the race card.

Then they placed Deputy Kenny LaVallee on the stand. LaVallee testified that asking Kennedy if he had ever conducted a felony car stop violated a Lowell Police Department procedure under civility and that I violated "workplace safety" regulations. He said it was an inappropriate time to ask that question. Yet Buckley stated in his original report that "this was the right way to conduct a stop" (Buckley, Apr. 13, 2).

Additionally, LaVallee stated it was uncivil of me because Kennedy found what I said to be "unacceptable to him." Basically, I should have known that Kennedy was sensitive and that what I said would make him cry. Speaking to him then, when he found it to be unacceptable, justified finding me guilty of conduct unbecoming to a police officer. In my mind I thought the whole thing reeked of discrimination. A minority officer can't ask a white officer a question that he feels is unacceptable, even if the white officer has acted out of line and put other officer's lives in danger. LaVallee's statements were so glaringly discriminatory it was ridiculous.

I had been to court to testify so many times at that point that I was familiar with the procedures and I walked out of court that day feeling confident that I had won. All the evidence clearly pointed towards the truth, that I had acted appropriately.

A month or so later, Sullivan called me to tell me that he had just received the commission's finding and that I lost. The commission decided in favor of the Lowell Police Department based on the perjured testimonies of LaVallee and Buckley. In its finding, the commission found that I was not a credible witness and the testimonies of LaVallee and Buckley were more "factual." The commission did lower my suspension from fifteen days to ten since Kennedy accepted ten days of extra duty as his punishment for the incident. They wanted to show there was no discrimination. I was not given any of my special assignments back, though. Still no SWAT, still no instructing, still no motorcycle duty.

"Okay," I replied resolutely. "You said that might happen. I need to file an appeal now, right?"

"No, that's not an option anymore. You have no right to an appeal, Bob."

"What do you mean?" I asked, completely thrown off by his response. "You told me I can appeal, and that most likely I would have to. What changed?"

"You lost that right, because you were found to not be credible," he responded.

"That's the law?"

"Yes, that's the law. Your case is over. You have lost."

I couldn't believe it. It appeared quite clear they lied and my testimony was supported by the written reports, but I was found to not be a credible witness so I couldn't appeal? It didn't appear right to me, but he was my lawyer and I had no reason to question what he had said.

The deadline to file the appeal came and went, and at that point the case was truly over. A couple of months later, I learned that I had been lied to when I spoke with another lawyer about my case.

"Why didn't you appeal?" he asked.

"My lawyer told me I couldn't."

"What!" he exclaimed. "That's crazy, you most certainly had a right to appeal."

I had a right to an appeal. Everyone has the right to appeal. Why did my lawyer lie to me? I believe it was because Davis had gotten to Gerry Flynn, the union president, and I think he told Sullivan to not allow me to appeal. From that point on, the police union that was supposed to protect me would continually be working against me.

The Bus Incident

About a year and a half after the Kennedy incident, in October of 1998, several officers from Massachusetts went on a union sponsored bus trip to Boston in order to attend a political rally (Rivera et al v. Lowell Police Department). A lot of the officers were from Lowell. John Leary invited female officer Vanessa Dixon, who was his ex-girlfriend, and she was the only female officer on the trip.

A group of officers on the trip became intoxicated, insulted the bus driver, and got into an argument on the ride home. This was problematic for several reasons, as a police officer is not supposed to drink to the extent of extreme intoxication, even while off duty. The nature of police work is such that you may be needed at any moment and you must always be in a condition where you can immediately work in an emergency. Additionally, we were required to act in a manner that would not cause the public to look poorly upon the police as an institution at all times. These rules were in our manual in Lowell and fairly standard rules for police officers everywhere.

The other main reason the event became notable is because some of the men harassed Dixon and made sexually explicit comments towards her to the point where she got off the bus and attempted to hitch a ride home. It appears the majority of the disturbance was between Leary and Dixon though. It was a quarrel between two ex-lovers and never should have escalated the way that it did.

Ed Davis was never one to miss out on an opportunity to get his way, though, and he worked hard to make it appear as though the incident was actually far worse than it was. He ultimately failed, but still ruined lives in the process. I believe he used the incident to clean out the department and get rid of some of the officers to whom he had taken a disliking. To me, it would appear as though there were men on that bus that Davis wanted to get rid of, and men who were just in the way of Davis' friends who he wanted to have move up.

The way the investigation was handled is a classic example of the way Ed Davis managed his command staff, and the scorn for the law and due process that existed for many of the men who worked with him. The investigation was not handled properly, and there is significant evidence to imply that Davis and his cronies manipulated the situation to their own advantage.

Throughout the course of the investigation, Vanessa Dixon and her sister, Robin Dixon, changed their stories multiple times, often after long, unrecorded interviews with Ed Davis. Davis formally met with Dixon on six occasions regarding the incident, and spoke to her about it many more times, but none of this was recorded or officially noted anywhere. Tousignant, as the main officer in charge of the investigation, denied requests by officers to have a union representative or attorney present during their interviews, which went against department rules and regulations (Rivera et al v. Lowell Police Department, P. 28). Vanessa Dixon was officially interviewed four times, but two of those interviews were not recorded, another violation of department policy. Most of the interviews were completed without notes or recording, which by its nature draws suspicion that manipulation occurred.

Officer Angel Otero, who was up for a promotion to Sergeant, was charged with sexual harassment even though Dixon never mentioned it and even denied that Otero had done anything wrong. Davis attempted to get Dixon to implicate Otero a number of times, but she refused. He pressed charges anyway, admitting later in court that he charged Otero, his brother, and another man, Officer Scotty Fuller, without a victim. Davis claimed that he hoped his investigation would yield a victim at some point in the future. It appears as though his standard method of investigation is "charge first, investigate later", as this was not the first time he did something like this in his career.

Officer Rivera, another Hispanic who was a detective in the drug unit, was charged with lying, sexual harassment, and creating a hostile work environment.

At the beginning of the investigation, based on the original testimonies given, there was no evidence to implicate that Officer Gerald Flynn had done anything that would allow Davis to formally charge him. After meeting with Davis, Dixon changed her testimony and claimed he said "fuck" several times. This was enough to charge him.

Almost a year after the incident, in August 1999, Dixon had another unrecorded interview with Ed Davis. After this meeting was over, she contacted Buckley and changed her testimony again, reporting that Officer Pender, who had not yet been implicated, had exposed himself to her. The Appellant's attorneys were not made aware of the fact that Dixon had issued this statement, even though it was required by law. Buckley claimed it was because he did not think Dixon planned to testify to the fact that Pender exposed himself until a month later, a mere three days before the trial was to begin. This is when the Appellant's attorneys were informed of this change, and given all of Buckley's reports on the incident. Pender was a Hispanic detective on the drug unit who also knew about some of Davis' favored employees engaging in corrupt activity.

Dixon mentioned that Ed Davis told her to figure out a way to implicate Officer Flynn (Rivera et al v. Lowell Police Department, P. 21), and he repeatedly pushed for several other officers, including the Otero brothers and Pender, to be implicated in the incident in some way as well even though they were not really involved. It seems she eventually gave in to his demands.

Dixon was never punished for being intoxicated on the trip, or for lying. None of the other officers on the bus who got intoxicated were punished for intoxication or misconduct either (Rivera et al v. Lowell Police Department, P. 27-28). It appears as though only the officers who were Hispanic or had crossed Davis in some way were punished. Some of these men were implicated by Vanessa Dixon, possibly at Davis' request; some of these men were found to have done no wrong.

The initial hearing occurred in front of the city manager, Brian Martin, and all of the charges were upheld for everyone except Officer Flynn. The punishments given out ranged from six months suspension to termination. All the men who were detectives lost their positions and Otero and Fuller were bypassed for promotion. When the case went to appeals, almost all the charges were dropped and almost all the punishments were reduced, but the damage had been done. No one got their positions back and the promotions had already been given to other people. Was this his plan all along?

The effort to punish Flynn managed to attract some negative attention, although it didn't affect Davis too badly. The civil service commission found that the city had "no firm evidence ... and suggests there was a concerted effort by the administration to punish the head of the patrolmen's union" (Wickenheiser), and several newspaper articles accused Davis of unfairly targeting Flynn in the investigation. What exactly did Flynn do to make Davis mad?

Davis was not the only one who acted improperly during this investigation. Buckley, who had been promoted to Lieutenant by this point, was given the responsibility of managing the case for the Lowell Police Department. He violated the sequestration order that was put in place by discussing testimony of Robin Dixon with Vanessa Dixon and her attorney. Sequestration orders are put in place to ensure the integrity of the testimony, and by violating this, the testimony of the Dixon sisters was pulled into question. From the appeals court's conclusion:

> Lt. Buckley's involvement cannot be overlooked. He was assigned to manage this case for the Appointing Authority. His actions allowed and encouraged Dixon to perjurer herself time after time. Buckley's actions show a flagrant disregard of the law and the process (Rivera et al v. Lowell Police Department, P. 20).

This is the type of officer that Buckley is. This is the type of officer that Ed Davis holds in high regard. This is how the department in Lowell, Massachusetts, is run.

Otero would have been the first minority officer to be promoted to sergeant in the history of the police department. Davis passed him and Officer Fuller over due to the trumped up investigation that was currently being held against them. Fuller was the union vice president and was a stand-up, honest cop, so he obviously was not suitable for command staff in Lowell.

Davis chose to promote one of his friends, Kelly Richardson, instead. Otero and Fuller filed civil lawsuits against the city. During the court proceedings of this case, Davis stated that an additional factor for bypassing Otero and promoting Richardson was that Otero, as a minority, had poor communication skills.

"Angel Otero speaks two languages. How many do you speak?" Vincent Dicanni, Otero's lawyer, asked Davis.

"One, but I don't see how that matters," Davis huffed.

"And when Richardson called a female employee a cunt (Rivera et al v. Lowell Police Department, P.34), you considered that as a superior communication skill?"

Again, Davis couldn't answer.

Otero had been a staff sergeant in the U.S. Army and served as a tank commander. Richardson was just a close friend of Davis. At some point the city settled, and Otero and Fuller were promoted several years later. Richardson is now a captain. His brother is the Chief of the Dracut Police Department, which is a town neighboring Lowell. Another nepotistic recurring coincidence with police families is family members holding positions of high authority in police agencies throughout the region.

Years after this happened, Otero said, "I feel that the chief ruined my career because he charged me with all these bogus charges, and there was not one person on that bus that could say I did anything wrong ... including Vanessa Dixon" (Alvarez vs. Lowell, P.140).

That's what Davis did. He ruined the careers of other men, ruined the lives of other men, in order to meet his goals. Otero was the first Hispanic officer who did well enough on the test to make it to the top of the promotion list. Davis "passed over Otero because of the allegations that were made against him by a female African-American police officer who said he sexually harassed her

..." (Alvarez vs. Lowell Jan 26, 2007, P. 111). Except, that was a lie. She never said he harassed her. Davis charged him without a victim. Davis claimed that he knew Otero had sexually assaulted someone, and it was just a matter of time before the truth came out. If he continued with his investigation, he said, a victim would somehow appear. Vanessa Dixon was interviewed dozens of times by Davis as he tried to get her to accuse Otero of wrongdoing, in spite of her repeated refusals to implicate him.

This is the same method Davis had been accused of using years ago to get rape victims to identify an innocent man as their rapist. It seems as though Davis has effectively used this method of solidifying accusations throughout his whole career. It's worked well for him, and has become his "go to" mode of operation. I consider Ed Davis to truly be the Bernie Madoff of law enforcement.

When Davis realized the he couldn't get the sexual harassment to stick, he ordered Officer Joe Zanolie to conduct surveillance on Otero for possible drug dealing. Once again there were absolutely no signs that Otero ever used drugs, let alone sold them. He kept Otero under investigation anyway.

Vanessa Dixon sued the police union and individual officers involved after this incident was over. She claimed a variety of misdeeds; retaliation, discrimination, and sexual harassment. She won $2.2 million along with retirement benefits and compensation for lost wages (Vanessa Dixon v. Lowell Retirement Board).

Corruption, Cronyism, and Discrimination

INTERNATIONAL BROTHERHOOD OF POLICE OFFICERS

A DIVISION OF THE NATIONAL ASSOCIATION OF GOVERNMENT EMPLOYEES, AFL/CIO

159 Burgin Parkway, Quincy, MA 02169

(617) 376-0220 Fax (617) 376-0285

August 18, 1999

City Manager Brian J. Martin
City of Lowell – Lowell City Hall
375 Merrimack Street
Lowell, Massachusetts 01852

Dear Mr. Martin:

As stated in my two previous letters to you dated May 26, 1999 and August 2, 1999, the issue of disparate treatment as it relates to certain members of the Lowell Police Department, particularly patrolmen, has now reached epidemic proportions. In fact, the Superintendent of Police has not only has allowed this to fester, but has condoned this type of behavior by his unwillingness to take appropriate action against those responsible for such indiscretions. As I so vigorously tried to impress upon you in my last two letters, *"favoritism and cronyism"* emanates from the Office of the Superintendent of Police. However, your own lethargic method of rubber stamping any matter concerning this administration is just as problematic. Moreover, as the appointing authority, you are ultimately responsible for the unsafe, hostile, and retaliatory work environment that has become the Lowell Police Department.

As I stated in my previous correspondence, we will no longer sit back and allow our members to become "sacrificial lambs" by an administration that condones racism, bigotry, and prejudice. This is rather ironic considering the fact that the Superintendent was recently quoted in the *Lowell Sun* as opposing the very entity in which we speak. In fact, Deputy US Attorney General Eric Holder was the guest speaker at this event in which the Superintendent denounced racism by police officers. In reading the article published by the *Lowell Sun*, I didn't know whether to laugh or to vomit after reading the comments and quotes of the Superintendent of Police. The fact that the Deputy US Attorney General is an African-American was the only reason the Superintendent broached this issue. His common compulsion to deceive those who are unfamiliar with his real management style is disgraceful.

Moreover, every one of the over 60-plus members of the Superintendent's command staff, his supervisory staff, and his civilian management team are W-H-I-T-E. The fact that not one Superior Officer or any member the Superintendent's civilian management team is of color speaks volumes about the management of the Lowell Police Department. Our recent distinction as an *All-American City*, was in large part the result of our ethnic and cultural diversity. However, it is sinful that the Lowell Police Department doesn't practice what we preach!

I mention this because I have had the distinct honor of meeting the Honorable Deputy US Attorney General Eric Holder on a number of occasions. In fact, we both recently testified before a subcommittee of the House Judiciary Committee regarding the issue of gun control. I also told the Deputy Attorney General about wide spread corruption within the hierarchy of the Lowell Police Department and how the US Attorney's Office and the FBI interviewed several members of the Lowell Police Department, including superior officers, regarding this issue. Although several members of this department were granted immunity from prosecution and admitted to personal knowledge of criminal activity by high-ranking members of this administration, including the Superintendent of Police, nothing has ever been done to those who are responsible for these illegal acts.

• Page 2 August 18, 1999

In fact, those of us who had the courage to come forward are now being targeted for discipline and retaliatory treatment by this administration. My obvious attempts to convince you, the appointing authority, of the seriousness of these matters appear to have fallen upon deaf ears. The retaliatory treatment to which we have been subjected is nothing short of harassment; in fact we are victims of an administration bent on vengeance. This obvious retaliatory treatment is in direct violation of the *"Federal Whistle Blower Act"* and we intend to pursue every legal avenue afforded to us under the United States Constitution. However, as a last ditch effort, I implore you to finally address and investigate these issues and not to simply rubber-stamp the findings and conclusions of the Office of the Superintendent of Police.

It is also common knowledge that the Superintendent continues to "portray" a close and personal relationship with the US Attorney General, Janet Reno, as well as other members of the US Justice Department. In fact, he stated during several roll calls that he had a letter from the US Justice Department stating there was no investigation into widespread corruption within the Lowell Police Department. He even once boasted during a verbal argument with a civilian in City Hall, *"Do you think Janet Reno would investigate me?"* It is this type of arrogance that emanates from the Office of the Superintendent of Police and filters down from the Command Staff. As someone who knows the Attorney General personally, I do not believe she is even remotely aware of the type of illegal acts I described, but rather another example of bravado on behalf of the self-absorbed and self-professed "Godfather of Community Policing."

Enclosed are copies of reports of the most recent incident involving a minority Officer and the disparate treatment he has received as a member of this police department. As you are aware, this Officer is also an African American who has continuously received lip service by this administration regarding documented activity of racism and harassment. This is to inform you of the serious nature of these charges and to ensure that you are fully aware of the incidents this Officer so painfully articulates in dramatic detail. This will be the last time I will address this issue with you. However, I will continue to follow-up these matters with the appropriate state and federal authorities. This is not to be misconstrued as a veiled union threat, but rather a final desperate attempt to compel you to take action. The same type of action you took when several high-ranking members of the patrolmen's association were alleged to have committed similar acts. They were removed from their positions, transferred to other shifts and ridiculed in the news media before they even were interviewed or charged with any departmental violations.

Furthermore, this is not an isolated incident involving racism and bigotry within the Lowell Police Department, but rather a long and repulsive history, which is only addressed when it suits the political agenda of the Superintendent of Police. In fact, additional evidence to support these assertions are the various complaints filed with Equal Employment Opportunity Commission (EEOC), the Massachusetts Commission Against Discrimination (MCAD), the Massachusetts Labor Relations Commission and the Massachusetts Board of Conciliation and Arbitration regarding these types of improprieties. In closing, I hope you will finally address this issue and not simply "whitewash" this as a Union / Management dispute. Moreover, we believe that your failure to address this issue in a timely and professional fashion could have dire consequences as it relates to the millions of dollars the Lowell Police Department receives in state and federal grants, thus jeopardizing the livelihood of many fine and dedicated police officers.

Sincerely,

Gerald J. Flynn, Jr.
President, IBPO Local #382
IBPO National Vice President

Cc: IBPO Local # 382 Membership
IBPO Attorney Michael Williams
IBPO Attorney Richard K. Sullivan
IBPO National Executive Secretary
IBPO National President Kenneth T. Lyons
American Civil Liberties Union
US Deputy Attorney General Eric Holder
US Attorney General Janet Reno
Lowell City Solicitor Thomas Sweeney
Lowell Mayor Eileen Donoghue

My experience was that Davis ran his department on fear. As stated in the above letter, anyone who "had the courage to come forward" and address the "favoritism and cronyism" that "emanated" from Davis' office was "targeted for discipline and retaliatory treatment." This became clear during my court case when no one other than Davis' brother would come right out and expose his lies by telling the truth, in spite of the mountain of paperwork I had proving otherwise. Time and time again, the fear Davis instilled in people because of the way he retaliated against people who crossed him, becomes a prominent factor in his career. How many of those people were the men who were targeted by Davis during the bus incident?

In August 1999, Gerald Flynn wrote a letter on behalf of the International Brotherhood of Police Officers. In the letter, Flynn states that "several members of this department ... admitted to personal knowledge of criminal activity by high-ranking members of this administration, including the superintendent of police." After it was delivered, Flynn was served with an injunction where he was not allowed to speak on the topic again. He stepped down as union president shortly after and never followed through on his threat to expose the department.

What kind of criminal activity was he talking about? There is no way to know for sure due to the fact that Flynn was somehow effectively silenced by Davis and his cronies. However, an examination of the careers of the men discussed in this book will provide enough examples of criminal and corrupt activity to give his accusations credence. Maybe the crimes he speaks of were among the many discussed in this book, or maybe Flynn was privy to knowledge that I was not. There are plenty of instances of criminal activity from which to choose, and a few examples follow.

One of the ways that Davis managed to influence public perception in his favor was by manipulating the local newspaper, *The Lowell Sun*. Jack Sheehan, the chief before Davis, did not allow the press access to the police at all. If he found out officers in the department spoke to the press, they would be reprimanded (Thacher). He kept the place closed up tight, despite cries to do otherwise.

One of the first things Davis did as chief was to promote an open-door working relationship between the department and the *Sun*. Davis contacted a reporter, Patrick Cook, and gave him full access to the department. As an old friend of Davis, he was hired on as the communications manager for the Lowell Police Department (Thacher). As a result, it appears the *Sun* wrote the stories Davis wanted, the way he wanted them to be written.

It was a great opportunity for Cook, and he surely jumped at it. What local reporter wouldn't want exclusive access to a police department that had been previously closed to the media? One of the first articles Cook wrote praised Davis for opening up the department to the public. In it, Cook discussed how wonderful it would be for the department now that they had a working relationship with the local newspaper. Cook was one of the primary writers for all articles related to the department while Davis was Chief.

Deputy Superintendent Cormier was part of a group of command staff officers who arranged to have drunk driving charges against one of their friends dropped (Scott, Date Unknown). The operating under intoxication (OUI) charge was changed to protective custody. This is used when a person is intoxicated and cannot care for himself/herself. It is not a criminal charge, but it does appear on your record.

The officers were caught under the charge of obstruction of justice and they all received some type of discipline that would be considered extremely lenient in most departments. There was no reduction in rank or specialty position. In most departments, they would have been fired, but Lowell isn't most departments. No one received a punishment as harsh as my punishment for the incident with Kennedy.

The most ridiculous punishment was the one given to Cormier. It actually attracted negative publicity from the newspaper (Scott), in spite of the relationship with Cook, because the discipline was so extremely lax. Cormier was given a suspension without pay as punishment for manipulating police criminal records to help a friend; however, he was allowed to take it whenever it was convenient for him. He ended up serving his suspension during a planned family vacation.

In October 1997, there was a murder that took place in Lowell. A woman was found murdered in her bathtub, with blunt force trauma to her head and neck. Whenever there is a crime scene like this, the police cordon off the area, and anyone who comes and goes has to be signed into the crime scene logbook to show that they were inside the scene, and to identify when they were there. This is to help ensure the evidence is not disturbed by random people coming and going.

This particular murder scene proved to be of interest to Ed Davis and his friends, and he brought a group of civilian women in and out several times. The logbook showed that people came in and out of the crime scene forty times. Davis put the case at risk with his behavior, treating this homicide scene like it was a circus sideshow for his entertainment.

Sergeant Timmy Kilbride came to the precinct I was at after leaving the crime scene. I remember he looked stressed.

"That crime scene on Upham Street is a disaster. Davis has all these people coming and going in and out of there. It's a mad house."

It was rumored that Davis got a call from the DA's office in response to the way he handled that crime scene. As the Chief of Police, he had to be told that type of behavior was unacceptable and that he couldn't do it anymore.

Currently, there is an active federal investigation against a Lowell Vice cop, Thomas Lafferty, who used an informant to plant drugs on people. He made use of this informant for over a decade, reporting that he used the informant about 50 times and managed to make an arrest about 75% of that time (Rezendes).

Lafferty and the informant were exposed when the informant decided to sell his services to the state police to make more money. During his interview with them, he bragged about his ability to "plant" things (Scott, 2013). The state police immediately decided not to work with him and they sent out a notification that no other department should work with him either. An investigation into Lowell's use of the informant was quickly launched and several cases were thrown out due to the informant's involvement.

Officer Mike Miles was an admitted drug addict who overdosed on cocaine while on duty but was not fired. There was also a report that Miles had stolen drug evidence. Davis chose not to investigate or punish Miles, but he did admonish the reporting officer. Miles was in the Housing Unit with me in 1996, where he often left his assignment for four to six hours to go to Dracut where I was told he was having an affair with some woman. We reported his absence to our supervisor, but no action was taken. Miles later taught in the Lowell police academy about his experience with drug addiction as a police officer. This entitled him to extra points on the sergeant's exam. Meanwhile, my instructor experience and SWAT team leader experience was not credited because it wasn't in an academy environment.

Then there was Officer Geoffroy, who sold the Vice Unit secret radio frequency to a drug dealer for cocaine. Davis again chose not to investigate or punish, Geoffroy went to rehab and came back to his normal duties afterward. There is no such thing as accountability; as you will see from the examples in this book, if you're connected, you can do whatever you wish.

There are many more instances of criminal activity by Davis and other officers in Lowell that will be discussed throughout this book. There are just so many crimes to choose from that we can only speculate on what Flynn was threatening in his letter.

The main purpose of the letter from Flynn was not directed at the issues of criminal activity within Lowell, but rather an attempt to get them do something about the "long and repulsive history" of "racism and bigotry" in the department. This is the part of the letter to which Davis chose to respond, probably because it was forwarded to several people with whom Davis worked in the federal government and he couldn't get away with doing nothing. Shortly after Martin received the letter, Ed Davis organized a meeting for all the minority officers in the department. I received a written invitation that identified me as a minority officer, although Davis would later claim that he never saw me as such. In his letter, Davis claimed the meeting would be an open forum to discuss the issues of racial disparity within the department. I attended, curious of his intentions. Would he actually attend to some of the many issues present within the department?

Unfortunately, it quickly became clear to myself and many of the other officers there that the meeting was a complete sham. Davis spent the majority of the meeting assuring us over and over again that he wasn't racist. Then he went around the room and asked everyone how they felt about the way minorities were treated in the department. When Angel Otero started talking about how he was treated and about getting passed up for a promotion, Davis shut him up immediately, saying something like, "That kind of talk isn't what we're here for," Davis said. "If you keep it up, I will have you removed (Robert Alvarez v. City of Lowell, Jan. 11, 2006, P. 94)."

After that, it was difficult to go on. It was apparent that we weren't really there to have an open and frank discussion about issues of racial disparity. Still, the meeting managed to totter on. Some officers pointed out they were tired of being referred to as, "fuck ups" by white supervisors in the department. They felt it was unacceptable to be spoken to like that. What I said to Kennedy was unacceptable to him, but I never called him a "fuck up." As far as I know, no white officer's career ended because a minority felt it was unacceptable to be spoken to rudely. I left shortly after that, before the meeting was over, because I was completely disgusted.

I later found out that it was decided after I left that a minority would be assigned to the Command Staff in the Lowell Police Department. This person would be a liaison between the minority officers and the heads of the department. All of the officers present wanted to vote on the person who would be given this position, but Ed Davis insisted on choosing the individual himself (Robert Alvarez v. City of Lowell, Jan. 11, 2006, P. 94-95). He nominated Larry Hickman, who was completely distrusted by the other minority officers in the department due to his close relationship with the Chief. No one was going to go to him for assistance.

According to the post meeting memo that Davis sent out to all of us, officers discussed occasions where they had been treated unfairly or received negative comments from white supervisors.

Davis wrote that there was discussion over discipline being meted out unfairly, and it "was cautioned that there is danger in making assumptions based on the rumor mill" (E. Davis, personal communication, September 10, 1999). The conclusion of the meeting, according to Davis, determined that there is in fact "subtle" but serious discrimination in the department and everyone in attendance agreed that the officers needed a safe place to air their concerns without fear of retaliation.

The memo also outlined an action plan that was apparently based on recommendations and conclusions from the meeting. The department would hold monthly meetings with an Advisory Committee of ten to twelve members of the department to "discuss issues and develop solutions." Davis also agreed to meet with superior officers to discuss racial issues, to develop training on racial policies, and to review the promotional process to ensure decisions were not made based on race. None of the promises were fulfilled, other than Hickman receiving a position on Davis' staff. This was an insubstantial step because, as far as I know, no one ever approached him with any issues. The Advisory Committee was never created, and there were no trainings or reviews done to improve race relations in the department.

A few weeks later, Davis sent out letters inviting us all to another meeting. I chose not to go back, as I saw right through it and believed that Davis had no intention of making any real changes.

Deposition

The truth about the Kennedy incident was systematically buried by Davis and the city, and I came to realize that justice was never going to be served in regard to what happened. It had been well over a year, and Kennedy still had not suffered any consequences other than a few punishment duty days, while I lost several special assignments that had not been returned to me. On February 9, 2000, I filed a criminal complaint application against Kennedy for assault and battery against a police officer, hoping that further action on my part would force the issue and Davis would have to actually conduct a real investigation.

After filing, I expected that Kennedy would be placed on administrative leave. Past practice in the department put all officers charged with crimes on leave until the case is resolved. As far as I know, Kennedy was the only officer to ever continue working in the Lowell Police Department with criminal charges pending. There was never any official police investigation into the criminal charges I filed against Kennedy, it was all handled within the department. Kennedy was actually promoted to sergeant while the criminal charges I filed were still pending. Davis said that he didn't take the investigation seriously because my accusations were made up and thus should not prevent Kennedy from receiving a promotion. Yet Davis made up accusations to keep Otero from promotion. My valid allegations were not significant enough to keep Kennedy from moving up, ultimately robbing me of the promotion to sergeant. The hypocrisy is staggering. It's amazing how often Davis accuses others of doing the exact things he has done himself.

When the case against Kennedy was heard at the Lowell District Court, the charges were dismissed due to lack of evidence. Because my testimony was the evidence, my attendance was a crucial part of the case. I was not informed of the date of the hearing, thus I was prohibited from testifying. Once again, it was clear to me that they were going to continue to punish me and I was going to have to continue to fight.

Davis did do one thing, he responded to my charge by removing my locker from the patrolmen's locker room so that it was no longer close to Kennedy's (Robert Alvarez v. City of Lowell, Jan. 26, 2006, P. 42). I was reassigned to a locker with a broken lock out in the hallway. The message was loud and clear: if you question what I do, you will be punished. I obviously could not store my things in a locker with a broken lock, and I never used a locker in the station again for the remainder of my career. I actually found it safer not to keep one. There were numerous rumors about the Vice Unit under Davis planting drugs on people, and I was always concerned that they would plant drugs or stolen property in my locker so they would have an excuse to fire me. They were doing whatever they could to discredit me and I did not want to give them the opportunity to ruin my life even more.

In 2013, after I retired, there was the scandal about the informant who bragged to the State Police about his ability to "plant things," so my concern was not unfounded (Rezendes). They actually were planting drugs on people, it wasn't just a rumor.

A week after filing the criminal complaint against Kennedy, my case was also filed with the Massachusetts Commission Against

Discrimination (MCAD), this time with a different lawyer who was not from the union. I became hopeful that something would come from that as I was doing everything I could think of to expose the truth and get my career back on track. My lawyer scheduled a deposition with Davis. A deposition is a legal process where an individual gives sworn testimony as evidence, either written or oral. It is given before a court case goes to trial and the lawyers from both sides use it to determine the elements of the case.

From observing Deputy Lavallee and Sergeant Buckley lie on the witness stand during the civil service trial, I was expecting that Davis would lie on some level, too, but I still didn't understand the extent of corruption that existed within the city, and I did not expect the litany of lies to be as complex as they were. When I received a copy of Davis' deposition, I was completely shocked and awed at the monumental levels of lying to which he stooped. The deposition is given under oath under penalty of perjury, and Davis committed perjury over and over again. He just went on and said whatever he wanted to make me look like a bad guy, with no concern for what was a fact or what was the truth.

Davis began by stating that the incident between myself and Kennedy had been subject to an Internal Affairs investigation, and that disciplinary measures were taken only after the Internal Affairs investigation was complete. He said that he used the findings from a report sent to his office to determine his decision (Davis, Dep. 13-14, 17-18, 109-110). However, there was never an Internal Affairs investigation into the incident between myself and Kennedy. I had been informed of my upcoming suspension and had my instructor and SWAT team positions removed less than 48 hours after the incident, before Davis had even received reports from all the officers who were there.

He also said the original recommendation for punishment was the same for myself and Kennedy (Davis, Dep. 16), but this, too, was a lie. Davis claimed he ultimately reduced Kennedy's punishment because he apologized for his actions and that my refusal to take any responsibility for the incident was why my punishment was ultimately harsher (Davis, Dep. 14-15). During the civil service hearing and then in the trial, Kennedy never testified that his actions were inappropriate in any way. There was no acknowledgement that anything he had done was wrong. There was never an apology.

Kennedy was not removed from any special positions when the incident occurred, because he was not on any. He was removed from riding the motorcycle for a short amount of time while I was blocked from riding for long after. The incident never prevented him from moving forward with his career either. Later court documents would note that he managed a "meteoric rise" (Alvarez vs. Lowell) within the department in the years that passed after the incident, while I continued to have opportunities for advancement denied me.

Davis claimed that I had been identified as the aggressor in the incident between myself and Kennedy (Davis, Dep. 17), but none of the reports backed up that statement. He stated that he felt I had "endangered other police officers because of (my) behavior that day" (Davis Dep. 132). Kennedy was the only one who put officers at risk that day, by yelling and swearing the way he did during the felony car stop and then physically attacking another officer.

When he was asked about the criminal case I filed against Kennedy, he initially said he had not taken any action as a result of the case being filed, claiming that he believed the charges were unfounded. When pressed further, he admitted to moving my locker and issuing an order for Kennedy and me to stay away from each other, showing that he believed the charges had enough merit for him to do something (Davis, Dep. 20-21). If he truly believed the charges were unfounded, he wouldn't have done anything at all.

Davis testified that he spoke with a number of people before deciding to remove me from the SWAT team, and that my supervisors and the head of the Special Operations Unit (SWAT) "concurred with his decision to remove" me (Davis Dep. 127). He also testified that Roarke told him I had an attitude problem (Davis, Dep. 128-129). Neither of these things were true, my supervisors all wanted me back on the team.

Davis also brought up two events that had never been brought to my attention before; things that I had apparently done that, in combination with the Kennedy incident, were the basis for Davis removing me from some of my specialty positions. The first of these events revolved around an interaction that I had with a State Trooper. The second involved the death of a very close friend of mine where I was accused of desecrating his dead body. Davis claimed that my behavior during these incidents troubled him, and it became the basis of his defense against me as we moved forward. However, his recollection of these events were his own fabricated version of what happened and by definition more aligned with fantasy than based in fact. Much like the Kennedy incident, it was entirely false.

In 1996, Davis set up a program with the State Police that was meant to be mutually beneficial for both organizations. What the program was or what its goals were was never explained to me, so I can't expand on that. I came into roll call one day and received orders to ride with a State Trooper, and that he would be my supervisor and trainer for my shift. I was shocked with this order, as it was a huge breach of protocol, but I went along with it because that was my job. As I left roll call, I was admittedly annoyed. I didn't understand what the purpose was behind the program, and I wasn't comfortable being supervised by another officer in a situation where we would typically be partners.

I got in the state cruiser with this white kid. We got to talking and I found out that he was still a rookie, he had four years on the job in comparison to my ten. Apparently, he was supposed to teach me how to do traffic stops even though I had approximately a hundred OUI arrests. At this point, I became pretty pissed off.

"I just want to be clear with you before we get started. I'm not happy with my orders today," I told the trooper as we drove off. "This whole thing just doesn't make sense."

I was pretty angry being put down and treated like a moron, and I wasn't going to take it lightly. "Normally, in a two-man car, the officers work as partners. How can you supervise me? You have no rank above me and you don't have any special training or instructor certification that would qualify you to be my supervisor."

"I wasn't aware that was the issue," he replied. "As far as I'm concerned, we're working as partners."

Even with that settled I was still fuming. My supervisors just handed me over to this trooper and basically told me to obey him. On the same night I rode with the trooper, another Lowell officer was assigned to ride with a trooper as well. This white officer was not instructed to be supervised by the trooper. Why was I instructed to be this trooper's pet and not the other Lowell officer? This was one of the most degrading and blatantly discriminatory incidents I was forced to endure at that point in the Lowell Police Department. Unfortunately, it wouldn't be the last.

The trooper and I worked together amicably the rest of the night, and had dinner together with a few other officers at the end of our shift. I thought that would be the end of it because we had worked out any potential issues between the two of us there, in the car.

When I showed up at the station for my next shift, I was called into Davis' office. He was very angry.

"Demoura just told me about you and your attitude while you were working with that trooper last night," he fumed. "You hurt that trooper's feelings and you have ruined my fuckin' program."

"What?" I asked, bewildered. "I hurt his fuckin' feelings?"

"Why didn't you just follow orders and let him supervise you?" Davis continued his rant.

"Because he's not qualified. He has no rank above me and no training as an instructor. He has a lot less experience than me and so we both agreed to work as partners. Just because he's a state trooper doesn't mean that he is qualified to supervise me. I've worked with state troopers before doing plain clothes gang surveillance and we worked as equal partners. They're not superior to us just because they're troopers. They ride the highway, write tickets, and book accidents. City cops work felonies, drugs, and violent crime. There is a huge difference."

Davis grew red, clearly displeased by my answer.

"You destroyed my program. There was a lot of fuckin' work that went into setting this up."

"Well, then I'll apologize to him if that will help."

"He's not the one who complained. He told another trooper who told another trooper who told a lieutenant. The lieutenant called and complained."

I was completely frustrated. I didn't even understand how a complaint that had gone through so many people before making it to Davis could even be considered valid, especially after the trooper and I had finished our shift amicably. Additionally, I knew that what Davis was telling me was a lie. My actions did not ruin his program. At roll call earlier, it was announced that the union president,

Gerry Flynn, had filed a grievance against Davis' trooper program. He received a complaint from another Lowell police officer who had been chosen to ride with a trooper that night, because it was a contract violation and a change in working conditions. This is what ended the program, but I was the one who he chose to blame.

I sat there, trying to organize my thoughts and respond when Davis piped up again. "Where is your loyalty?"

Without even thinking I just blurted out, "My loyalty is to the US Constitution and the American people."

Davis went berserk and started pounding his fist on the desk.

"What the fuck is that! What the fuck is that! You're supposed to be loyal to me ... me!"

My head was spinning. Where the hell was I? I felt like I was in a foreign country. Apparently I did not know what loyalty was in Lowell. When I was a platoon sergeant in the Marine Corps, I received annual fitness reports that evaluated twelve characteristics. One of these characteristics was loyalty. For the three years I was a sergeant, my loyalty was characterized and listed as "outstanding." I knew what true loyalty was and Davis would never have mine.

There was definitely something more going on here than what meets the eye. By past practice, policy, and protocol, two officers of the same rank working together always work as equal partners. The only time this does not apply is if one officer is certified as a training officer in the FTO program for training new officers fresh from the academy, which was not the case here. There was no justifiable reason for this trooper to be in a position to train or supervise me. I protested this unofficial arrangement and the trooper and I settled the situation and it should have ended there. From the trooper's perspective, he didn't like the settlement because I wouldn't acknowledge his superior position over me, a position not supported by policy or procedure, but a position based on his feelings. When the State Police Lieutenant became aware of the situation, he felt the issue needed to be addressed so he called to complain about me.

Captain Demoura and Davis concurred with the trooper and his Lieutenant. They believed it was necessary to correct my attitude because I should have known I was inferior to the trooper. Because the rule that minority officers are inferior is actually an unwritten rule, Davis and Demoura could not address the issue directly. There could be no official reprimand because this unwritten rule was actually discrimination.

That was pretty much it; I left his office and the State Trooper program ended. I was surprised to find out that it was an issue during Davis' deposition.

Davis didn't just accuse me of refusing to obey orders and ruining the State Trooper program during his deposition. He completely fabricated a story of the events that evening. Davis actually said that the trooper and I "had a verbal altercation, and then Alvarez demanded to be taken back to the station" (Davis, Dep. 54). Once at the station, Davis claimed that I told my supervisor that I refused to participate. Davis said that he had to call me into his office and personally order me to participate in the program that night. He accused me of being insubordinate and rude to him, and that I was "very disrespectful" during the conversation (Davis, Dep. 60-66).

This was a complete and total lie. I never returned to the station and I never refused to participate in the program. The conversation between myself and Davis never happened that night because he was home for the night by the time I started my shift. The conversation with Davis actually happened as I was coming into the station for my next shift, after my shift with the trooper had been completed.

Ed Davis was so used to fabricating stories to suit his needs however, that I shouldn't have been surprised.

The other incident that Davis used as his reason for punishing me so harshly after the Kennedy incident involved a close friend of mine. Ed Davis accused me of desecrating his dead body. This man, Bob Marchionda, was a North Reading K-9 cop and on the SWAT team with me. We went hiking and mountain climbing together, our wives knew each other, and we helped each other out regularly.

Before his death, Bob had gone on a hiking and climbing trip with couple of other SWAT cops in the White Mountains in New Hampshire. It was a trip I had done with them a number of times in the past, but this time I wasn't able to go. I was at work, instructing a police motorcycle class, when I got a call from my wife.

"Bob, Denise's father just died. She can't tell him because he's up on the mountains somewhere. He isn't scheduled to be back until after the funeral."

I called Denise immediately.

"Denise, I have an idea about where they might be in the woods. If you want, I can go up to the mountains and see if I could find him and bring him back."

"I can't ask you to do that, Bob. Really, how are you going to find him just by guessing where he might be in that huge mountain range?

"Denise, I insist. I can find him. I know I can. I have to try."

It took a little convincing, but finally Denise gave in and said it was okay if I went.

I hung up the phone and got permission from my supervisor to leave work. I went home and packed a light 40 pound rucksack. Normally all the gear for a hiking trip was about twice that weight, but I knew I would have to be able to move quickly if I was going to have a chance of finding Bob. I eliminated as much as I could from the ruck, but there were some things that really were necessary for a hike in the White Mountains. The weather can turn on a dime up there, and I didn't want to freeze to death if it did. Besides, I didn't know when I would find them, if it would happen the first day, the second day, or at all.

I figured they would be somewhere between Mount Kerrigan, Mount Guyot, and the Bond Cliffs in New Hampshire. These mountains covered a huge span of territory, but if they had run the circuit like we had in the past, I figured I could catch up to them near the Kerrigan notch.

I started driving north around 10 a.m. It was about a 135-mile drive to the entrance that was the closest to where he might be. I hiked up through the notch and headed to the Desolation Trail twelve miles in. As I hiked down a trail by a stream, I picked up the scent of cigars, and I knew I had found them because we were all cigar smokers. I came down on them over the ridge and everyone was totally shocked and surprised. They chuckled as I approached, thinking I just came out to join the climbing. I was out of breath when I got down to them.

"Bob," I blurted out. "I'm here to bring you back home. Your father-in-law just passed and Denise needs you." I stood, trying to catch my breath as they stared at me in shock. "The funeral is tomorrow and we don't have any time to waste. I need to get you back home."

I definitely killed the mood, but as soon as everyone got over their shock, they erupted into questions.

"How the hell did you find us?"

"When did you leave?"

"How fast did you drive?"

"Ha, how fast did you run?"

I told them quickly about my trip and they were in awe that I had managed the trip in just five hours. Bob stood silently as he took in the news of his father-in-law's death and got over the shock that I had made the trip to get him and bring him home. Once I got done answering their questions, Bob put his pack back on and we basically "force marched" back to the car. We made it back almost as fast as my hike in.

I was eager to get back and deliver Bob to Denise. At one point on the drive home, he turned to me.

"Hey, let's not end up like my father in law. You can slow down a little." I looked down at the speedometer and realized he was right and I slowed down. I got him home at about 9:00 that night.

Marchionda handed this letter to me at the next SWAT training session.

25 JUNE 1996

Bob,

Being the kind of guy that I am, it is easier for me to put my feelings down on paper than it is to speak them. I just want you to know how much it meant to me when you were there during a time of need for my family and I. Words can't describe how I feel about your actions. I know that friends like you are extremely rare in these times. In fact, you are much more than a friend, you are my brother. Your loyalty and generosity are the true signs of camaraderie. I hope you know that I will be there for you, as you were for me. It was hard for me to keep myself composed in front of you, Larry, and Franie; not just because of the bad news, but because of the sacrifice you made in order to get to me. Although I was deeply touched by your actions, I was not surprised. I know the kind of man you are.

I need you to do one more thing for me. I need you to thank Jemma on my behalf for her patience, selflessness, and understanding. It is women like her that lets us be the men we are. She is truly special and I have always known that she understands us so well.

Denise was moved beyond words, and she sends her love for you both. She will never forget your mission of compassion for her. You were truly a noble knight in shining armor.

In closing, let me tell you that everyone who heard the story of your deed was amazed. Many could not fathom the idea of someone hiking at high speed for 20 miles over mountainous terrain just to find a friend and bring him home; a friend who would've been home the next day. Only now do they start to understand the bond that we certain few have.

With all my respect and loyalty,

Bob Marchionda

Bob Marchionda

Bob Marchionda and I were more like brothers than friends, and I never would have done anything disrespectful toward him or his family. When Ed Davis tried to say that I desecrated his body, and that I engaged in behavior that was "occult-like" when Bob died, I was mortified.

Davis wasn't the only one that accused me of this either. He later managed to get the mayor of Lowell, Eileen Donoghue, to file an affidavit echoing the false allegations of misconduct stated by him. In her sworn statement, she stated that all my punishments were justified and fair because of the fact that I "desecrated the body of a dead police officer." Her belief was that this was the worst of my offenses and this would become the catchphrase tied to my name. In an MCAD case, it was standard protocol for everyone involved in the case to file affidavits stating their position. As the mayor, why would Donoghue have knowledge of my case? I'm guessing she thought she would just jump in and add her spin, probably at Davis' request. Everybody with a title got to state their opinion knowing that their title alone gave them veracity, and Donoghue's statements gave Davis' accusations against me more clout. Eileen Donoghue is now a Massachusetts State Senator for Middlesex County; her lies in my case did nothing to slow her career.

The lie that I desecrated Bob's body came about after the events that occurred around his funeral. Bob died on the way home from a hunting trip in Canada in October 1996. The plane he was on experienced engine failure and crashed. There were six men on the plane other than Marchionda. Four were Lowell officers: Dave Seamans who was on SWAT with me, Lieutenant Steve Smith, Donnie Brill, and retired Sergeant John Sullivan. There was also the pilot, and one other person. Everyone on the plane was killed, and it was a huge local tragedy that affected all of us greatly.

The plane crash was announced at roll call. The Lowell families all knew, but Marchionda was from North Reading. Had anyone notified Denise? My first reaction was to make sure that Bob was actually on the flight that had gone down. Once I confirmed that he had, in fact, been on the plane, I requested permission to leave work. I wanted to make sure that Denise found out about her husband's death properly, from the men who had worked beside him, instead of from the news or elsewhere. The entire SWAT team got together and we went to her house. She must have known what had happened when we all showed up like that; but at first, no one could talk. I thought Frank Roarke or Rick Jolly was going to speak to her, but they couldn't find their voices. After a few moments of heartbreaking silence, I spoke up.

"His plane crashed and there were no survivors."

I think at that point we all started crying.

The Lowell Police Department took over handling the logistics because most of the officers who died were from Lowell, and we were a bigger department. Officers were sent to Canada to aid in the investigation and to transport the bodies back to Massachusetts. The bodies were taken to an airplane hangar in Lawrence, Massachusetts; where we held a small ceremony before moving the caskets to individual hearses to transport them to the funeral homes chosen by the families.

I organized the arrangements for police motorcycles to escort each of the hearses as they transported the bodies from the hangar in Lawrence to the individual funeral homes. Since everything happened so suddenly, we weren't as organized as usual and the men arrived to the hangar without individual assignments. Many of them were not local, and I was quite busy figuring who should be assigned to each hearse and making sure they had the right directions. I was unaware of any problems or arguments happening inside the hangar concerning the caskets as they were moved to the hearses.

I later found out that there had been a disagreement over the way Marchionda's casket was to be transported. I heard about this all secondhand, and to be honest, it didn't make sense to me. Apparently, Bob had a premonition that he was going to die, but he thought that it was going to happen during a SWAT operation. According to Rick Jolly, he had asked to have his body transported in a SWAT van if he died. Some of the men on the team wanted to fulfill this wish and it caused a skirmish at the hangar.

By the time I had organized the motorcycle escorts, Marchionda's body was in the hearse and the whole incident was over. Even though I didn't know what it was about, I knew there had been some arguing and I was put off by the whole thing. This wasn't the time or place to be arguing; it was unprofessional. We then carried on and escorted the hearse to the funeral home as planned.

Once there, the SWAT team transferred Marchionda's casket to the SWAT van. The members of the team who were there sat in and around the van to drink beers and smoke cigars while telling stories about Bob in his memory. Because we were going to start drinking, I wanted to get rid of the motorcycle so I drove it back to the station and returned in my own car.

After Bob's funeral, Denise Marchionda sent a letter to Ed Davis, expressing her gratitude for the way we supported her and dealt with her husband's death.

Dear Superintendent Davis,

I am writing to again thank you for all your efforts in my husband's, (Officer Robert Marchionda), behalf. The Lowell Police Department and the N.E.M.L.E.C. T.P.F./S.O.U. Units could not have done anything more to support and recognize the honorable police officers who perished.

I especially want to thank Officer Bob Alvarez from your station for the support and courage he gave to me this past year. My father died suddenly in June, when my husband was on his yearly hiking trip. I could not reach him. As I told you when we spoke last, Bob Alvarez was heroic when he hiked (ran) up a mountain, found my husband, and brought him home in less than 15 hours, so that he could attend my father's funeral services. If he didn't do this, my husband would not know of my father's death, and he would have missed my father's funeral. Bob Alvarez also came to tell me about my husband's death on October 20, 1996. Although I knew Robert was dead when Bob Alvarez came to my door, I would not have wanted anyone else to be there for me that night. Bob and his wife Gemma, along with many S.O.U. members, stayed by my side and protected me from unwanted intruders, as well as supported me through the most crucial moments of that terrible week.

The brotherhood of police officers is unmatched. I have known the S.O.U. Team for many years, and it is indeed rare that a group of men would give their lives for each other. These men would - without question. This loyalty has forged a deep bond that cannot be broken. They did everything that my husband would have wanted for his funeral. Their send off was a tribute to the brotherhood and done through their respect and admiration for my husband. I will never be able to thank them enough.

All of your other officers who were coordinating, planning, and attending services were also outstanding. You have an excellent police force. Also, Fr. Jim Robichaud has been extremely helpful these past months. Thank you for including me in the services rendered even though my husband was not a Lowell Police Officer.

Again, thank you for all your efforts and considerations in making this difficult time more bearable.

Sincerely,

Denise Marchionda
12/26/96

Ed Davis tried to use this event as the reason for my removal from the SWAT team. In his deposition, he said that the casket was removed from the hearse on the way to the funeral home, and transported the rest of the way in the SWAT van (Davis, Dep. 73). As the motorcycle escort for the hearse, I never would have allowed this to happen. He also said that the event was ritualistic (Davis, Dep. 74) and left him concerned that the team was somehow involved in the "Occult." He backed up this claim by saying we had all gotten matching tattoos. While some of the men had gotten SWAT tattoos, it was not an activity in which we had all engaged, and I did not have one myself. After it was determined that I had no tattoos, the issue was dropped, but Davis still continued to express concern over the behavior of the team that day. A bunch of guys honoring the death of a fallen comrade is not concerning behavior, it is a natural response elicited by the closeness that the team had, and should have had, considering the fact that we often put our lives on the line for each other.

I did not participate in the argument to transport Marchionda's body in the SWAT van, and I did not participate in any type of cult-like activity regarding Marchionda's death. There was no one who could verify that I had participated in any of the activities that Ed Davis expressed concern about because I didn't. He claimed to have spoken with my supervisors on the SWAT team to confirm my involvement and that I was the main instigator of this disgraceful conduct (Davis, Dep. 77-78). However, those conversations never took place. He even went so far as to say that Lieutenant Roarke had expressed concern about my attitude when he never did. Roarke actually asked to have me reinstated to SWAT after Davis removed me from the team, more than once. He would not have done that if he were concerned about my attitude.

Davis never took any reasonable action to show he was really concerned about my mental stability other than removing me from my specialty positions. He still allowed me to work as a patrol officer in situations where a "mentally unstable" person should have been removed. He never required me to participate in any type of counseling, in spite of the fact that he was "deeply concerned" about my mental status. The only thing he did was smear my name at the

NEMLEC chief's meeting, which prevented me from transferring to other departments in the area; and remove me from SWAT while attempting to change the acceptance process so he could put his politically connected guys on the team.

After reviewing Davis' deposition, I had to sit back for a minute to absorb what had just happened. The first item addressed in the deposition is that Davis was directed to read and sign the waiver notary, under the pains and penalties of perjury. Christine O'Connor, the attorney for the city, was present, and she acknowledged that Davis read and signed the document. The deposition ends with Davis' signature under the heading "signed under the pains and penalties of perjury this date, April 20, 2000." After reading the deposition, I immediately looked up the definition and elements of perjury under Massachusetts criminal law. Davis had clearly committed perjury and was in violation several times in his deposition.

I felt like I needed to do something once again, although I wasn't entirely sure if it would work. Davis committed a crime and he needed to suffer the consequences of committing that crime. It wasn't right that he could go around saying and doing whatever he wanted without anything happening. I decided to contact the State Police Special Investigation Unit because it was its duty to investigate things such as this.

Previously, Dave Pender contacted the State Police and attempted to report that Buckley had stolen money from the Vice/Narcotics Unit, but they refused to investigate. I was concerned that the State would also blow me off, but I actually knew two command staff State Troopers in the internal affairs unit. One was a personal friend and a lieutenant, and the other was a major who was in charge of the unit. I had been in the Marine Corps with his brother and he was aware of my personal reputation. I hoped that this would give me a better chance.

When I called the lieutenant, she told me that Tom Reilly, the attorney general of Massachusetts, was aware of my request for an investigation. Reilly and Davis were friends, so I knew that Davis would quickly be made aware that I was reporting him.

The lieutenant put me in contact with Bruce Dean, the assistant district attorney of the Special Prosecutions Unit in Boston. Dean interviewed me in Boston on December 14, 2000. I provided copies of Davis' deposition and other supporting documentation to him. He looked everything over and then placed the paperwork on his desk as he looked at me.

"Bob, you need to understand that perjury isn't really a prosecutable crime. It's more like, mmm, adultery. There is a law against it, but nobody ever goes to court over it."

"Really?" I thought. I had just spent a significant amount of time doing research on perjury cases and there were several convictions that I read about, so I knew he was lying. In fact, in 2002, a Chief of Police in Houston was indicted for perjury when he lied about cussing at the officers he supervised during an internal investigation (My Plainview). This is paltry compared to the lies committed by Davis and the others.

He folded his hands and looked at me like someone would look at a child when explaining something to them that they thought they couldn't understand. "Frankly, no judge would even hear this case anyway."

I was absolutely on fire with anger, but I kept my cool. I wanted to go off on him, but I thought I might need his assistance in the future.

"This is a serious issue. There needs to be an investigation," I said

"Ok, we'll look things over and get back to you."

A few weeks later I received a letter in the mail from him that stated, "After careful consideration of the information provided and the applicable case law, there is insufficient evidence or facts to support a criminal investigation into the allegations" (B. Dean, personal communication, January 16, 2001). The key word here is "criminal investigation" as opposed to "criminal charges."

This is how it's supposed to work; I report a crime to his office and he in turn then conducts an investigation. Only upon conclusion of the investigation can you determine if a crime has been committed. Bruce Dean made the determination that my report of a crime didn't need to be investigated. As he said, a chief of police who lies under oath really isn't committing a crime anyway, right?

I believe that Bruce Dean couldn't do an investigation because it would leave a paper trail. His investigation would have to overlook or ignore the facts in order to clear Davis of any wrongdoing, and an investigation would put all of that into the official record. They couldn't risk that, it was easier to say my accusations had no merit.

Now they knew I planned to try to prosecute them for perjury if I had the chance, which would have an effect on my case later. Davis also now knew he had complete immunity from any type of criminal investigation while Dean and Rielly were around. Essentially, this established that he was now above the law. He probably believed he was completely free to lie about anything, because after that, he did.

Internal Affairs: Citizen's Complaints

When I didn't get anywhere with the State Police on prosecuting Davis for perjury, I filed citizen's complaints with Internal Affairs (Complaints 2000-073 to 2000-076). The Internal Affairs department was designed to deal with issues of police misconduct and violations of department policy. I needed to use this unit to address these issues, because in the real world that's supposed to be their job. I discovered that what these organizations were designed to do is very different from how they actually function. The Lowell Police Professional Standards Unit or Internal Affairs (I.A.) was the height of hypocrisy when I worked there, and I doubt anything has changed since I left.

Davis created I.A. after a lawsuit was filed against Buckley and another officer for beating a man who had extensive medical bills from the injuries he sustained. The plaintiffs' attorney pointed out that there was no unit in Lowell, and there was never an investigation. The city paid out a large sum of money for the case. Davis openly spoke of creating I.A. with the police union, and I was told that this was why Davis created it; to create the appearance of professionalism and to aid in the defense of future lawsuits.

After I.A. was created, the *Lowell Sun* advertised that the Lowell Police had an open door policy to the needs of the community and encouraged the public to file complaints if anyone believed an officer had engaged in misconduct. It was like opening flood gates, and citizens' complaints began to be filed constantly. I was very familiar with I.A. because over my years as an officer in Lowell, I had between twenty to thirty I.A. complaints filed against me. The majority of the complaints were from people I had arrested who complained the charges against them were unjust. People who I had found responsible for causing car accidents filed complaints stating that it really wasn't their fault.

To give an idea of how I.A. worked in Lowell, here is just one example of an I.A. investigation against me for misconduct. I responded to a car accident where a pedestrian was hit by a vehicle in traffic. Upon my arrival, the white male driver approached me and declared he was an attorney whose office was in the city and that I should respect his status. He announced that this whole accident was a scam by a homeless person to extort money from his insurance company. I asked him to hold on and let me do my investigation.

The Hispanic pedestrian was being loaded into an ambulance while I attempted to interview him. The lawyer hovered over me as I spoke to the victim, even after I asked him to step away and quiet down. He continued to interrupt me as I tried to speak to victim. I finally turned to the lawyer sternly.

"If you don't shut your mouth and return to your vehicle I will arrest you."

He reluctantly went back to his vehicle.

The victim stated he was crossing the street to return to his vehicle parked on the other side when he was hit. He went on to say he had just gotten out of the hospital a week ago after having surgery. When I ran the license plate of the vehicle parked across the street, the listed owner was the victim who went to the hospital.

After my investigation, I returned to the lawyer, who was now sitting in his car, to issue him a citation and crash report. He was completely incredulous and claimed that I only took the side of the victim because we were both Hispanic. He went on to say I was incompetent and only got my job because "they had to hire my kind." I sighed internally as I completed the paperwork because I knew this would result in another I.A. investigation.

The driver wrote in his complaint that I was "disrespectful." I had to write a follow up report as to why I cited the driver and was then subjected to a two-hour-long recorded interrogation in I.A. Sometime later I was exonerated. All of the complaints filed against me were for petty reasons, and I was exonerated in all cases, but it was always after an in-depth investigation.

I had a voluminous amount of use-of-force arrests where I utilized OC spray, PR-24 impact tools, and also fought with suspects where hospitalization for injuries was required, yet I never had one complaint filed for excessive use of force. Each case was so justifiable under the circumstances that no one ever complained. It was usually people who felt they shouldn't be charged with a crime who complained.

Even though my experience with I.A. had not been exactly positive, I needed to utilize any and all institutes or factions within the system to address and correct what had happened to me.

I filed a complaint against James Kennedy, Tommy Kennedy's father, stating my belief that he had abused his power as city solicitor to protect his son. I felt an investigation should be conducted to determine if, as the city solicitor, he had violated state law. Specifically, I believed he violated Mass General Law Ch268A, which deals with conflict of interest. Protecting his son from a proper police investigation was certainly a conflict of interest, and a man in his position should not be abusing that power. I then briefly cited the original incident with Kennedy and the numerous subsequent attempts by myself to ensure that the event was properly investigated.

I filed two complaints about the acts of perjury committed by Mark Buckley and Ed Davis when testifying about events concerning me. Davis' numerous lies have been discussed in detail above, and his continuing acts of perjury will be discussed further later. Buckley committed perjury by claiming that he witnessed what occurred between myself and Kennedy the night of the felony car stop. However, this was not possible because Buckley wasn't even on the same street as Kennedy and myself when the assault happened. Additionally, there were other officers who told me that Buckley had said he didn't really see what happened that evening because he wasn't there, and that he was going on what Kennedy had told him.

I also filed a complaint about the fact that I was never informed of the date of the hearing for my assault charges against Kennedy. As stated earlier, the charge was thrown out due to lack of evidence because I wasn't there to testify. I requested that the hearing be rescheduled and to have the venue changed to a different court where the Kennedy family did not have so much influence. I also requested to be informed of the time and date of the new hearing so that I could attend.

After filing these complaints, I received notice from the Lowell Police Department "that after a complete and impartial investigation" the department decided that my complaints were "unfounded" (W. Taylor, personal communication, May 9, 2001). Furthermore, it was "determined that the allegations contained in (my) Complaints were specious, frivolous, and imprudent" (W. Taylor, personal communication, May 9, 2001). I was accused of violating a few policies and procedures and threatened with discipline "up to and including termination" if I did it again.

The "impartial investigation" was probably completed by Davis himself as it never left the department (W. Taylor, personal communication, May 9, 2001), so it would have fallen under his authority. He officially decided that he had not committed perjury. Davis was allowed to investigate himself and decide if his actions could be attributed to any type of wrongdoing, which is a clearly absurd. When I filed the complaints, I was told that they would be investigated by the State Police to prevent a conflict of interest, but later found out that Davis had decided to keep the investigation in Lowell and under his charge. I shouldn't have been surprised because my effort to go through the State Police to have Davis investigated failed before. I was stuck using a system over which they had control, and I had to keep trying everything I could. I wasn't going to give up.

I spoke with Sergeant Kevin Sullivan, who was assigned to Internal Affairs, about my complaints, trying to get some answers.

"The complaint against James Kennedy was thrown out and never investigated," he said while looking over the files.

"What?" I asked. "Why?"

"Just because," he said.

I took a deep breath. "What about Buckley's perjury?"

"He said he didn't do it and he answered all of my questions right." Sullivan looked past me, refusing to make eye contact.

"Ok …" I don't know why I expected anything different, really. "Hey, while I'm here, do you have the incident report number from the I.A. investigation of the Kennedy incident?"

Davis testified to the existence of this report at length in his deposition, and I wanted to see it.

"There is no report number," he replied, again avoiding eye contact.

"Really? From my knowledge, all I.A. reports have a number assigned to them. So why doesn't the report have a number?"

"Well, uh, because there is no report," he responded. "Do you have any more questions?" His level of discomfort obviously increased the longer I was there. I had nothing else to ask, anyway. I had what I came for.

"No," I responded curtly. "Thanks for all the help."

Later, during the discovery phase of my case, I found that Tousignant and Sullivan had interviewed Lieutenant Laferriere as part of my complaint that Buckley had lied. The report by Sullivan stated that Laferriere cleanly and unequivocally stated Buckley told him that he wasn't present when the Kennedy assault took place and that Buckley said he didn't really know what happened (Lieutenant Laferriere Interview).

Captain Taylor pulled me into his office a few days after I got the determination back.

"Don't do this again, Bob, or you'll be fired."

"Don't do what again?"

"You know."

"No, I don't. Don't do what again?" I was trying to get him to say don't file any more complaints or you'll be fired but he just wouldn't say it.

"Just don't do this again," he repeated.

"Tell me what you mean. I don't know what you're talking about."

"If you don't know, I can't help you," he said, disgusted. "You're dismissed."

I was still putting together a case against the department. I now had concrete knowledge that Davis never conducted an Internal Affairs investigation and no report number existed. There was no documentation to back up his decision to suspend me. I originally thought Davis would cover his tracks by creating some false reports so he could at least have dates and a report number, but he either overlooked it or underestimated me. With no incident report number there was nothing he could use to cover up his lie. Davis had testified that there had been an investigation and that the result of the investigation had influenced his decision to suspend me and remove me from my special assignments in the sworn testimony of a deposition. He lied under oath and now I had proof.

Acting as My Own Attorney

Around the time that I filed my citizen's complaints, there were two sergeant positions coming up. The position was given to the person with the highest score on the list from the Sergeant's exam. If more than one person had the same score, the promotion was traditionally given to the person at the top of the list alphabetically. The exam consisted of a written, multiple choice test, with extra points added for experience in specific areas. For example, teaching positions in the academy added points. Unfortunately, all my teaching experience was outside of the academy so none of it counted. As I mentioned before, Mike Miles taught about his experience as a drug addict in the academy, and he received extra points on the exam, but my SWAT instructor position didn't count, and I received no extra points for any of my training roles.

That year, Kennedy scored an 86 and was tied with Stevie O'Neil at what was the top of the sergeant promotional list when the positions opened up. I was next with a score of 85. By all rights, Kennedy should have been fired for assaulting me and at the least ineligible for promotion. He also should have been under investigation for the criminal complaints I filed, but he was not. Just as Otero was bypassed for promotion, Kennedy should not have been eligible for promotion either.

Shortly after Kennedy was promoted to sergeant, he was assigned to the west sector and I was informed that I was no longer allowed to work in the east or west sectors of the city. This blocked me from working in over two thirds of the city. From what I was told, Kennedy complained to someone that he was afraid that he may have to supervise me. I guess they wanted to make sure I didn't make him cry again.

In Lowell, there is an annual union bid for patrolmen to pick their shift and position. I picked a cruiser patrol, Car-9, in the east sector, as I had done in the past. Once Kennedy got promoted, I was only allowed to take positions in the north sector, on the other side of the Merrimack River. This restricted work area order came down just after I chose an east sector cruiser. I was removed from the car and placed on a walking route in the north, an extremely undesirable position.

I sent a request to the union president, Dennis Moriarty, to file a grievance, but he refused. His claim was that Davis had "just cause" for my removal. Moriarty was a Davis crony who became the union president after Gerry Flynn was forced to leave. Sometime after my reassignment to the north sector, Moriarty attended a meeting Davis set up to make a determination about my employment with the city. Moriarty was supposed to represent me and my interests, because this was his job as the union president. At the end of the meeting Moriarty called me to meet up.

"Eddy Davis, John Cox and the city solicitor have decided that they are going to fire you," he said. Cox was the city manager then, and I am not sure which city solicitor he was talking about, but Tommy Kennedy's father, James Kennedy, was one of city solicitors at the time and I assume it was most likely him.

"On what grounds?" I asked, shocked and angry.

"All those complaints of corruption you filed. They're all false, which is very concerning behavior." He stopped for a moment and looked at me. "You should quit before they fire you."

"What the hell are you doing Dennis? You're supposed to defend me."

"Look Bob, you brought this on yourself. You can't get mad at me."

"Well, I'm not quitting. You let Davis know he can go ahead and fire me if he wants. But he better have reasonable grounds to do so."

I never heard another word from anyone ever again about being fired. It was the most pathetic scare tactic I had ever seen.

It wasn't long before Kennedy got promoted again to lieutenant, which took him off the street. I returned to Car-9.

Over the years, the issue of whether or not minority police officers should form their own separate union frequently arose. The response was usually, "there's no need for a separate union because minorities are not treated any differently than anyone else. Why are minorities always crying about being treated differently?" This is a common defense tactic; any time a person or group says they are being treated unfairly, the accused turns the accusation around on them in order to avoid a real conversation about the issues at hand.

My experience was that the union rarely worked to ensure I was given fair treatment. This is what happened when I was removed from Car-9, even though it was a contractual violation. The union should have protected me; instead, I was threatened with termination.

The first MCAD case I filed in December 1999 was never investigated. It sat at the MCAD for two and half years before it came to a conclusion in the summer of 2002. My lawyer filed the case stating several incidents of discrimination, but the city never addressed the accusations. It just submitted my birth certificate, which listed my race as white as though that was all that was needed to prove there was no discrimination. The MCAD report determined that I was white and not a minority. My case was dismissed. When I was born in 1958, the only options for birth certificates was white or black, and the term Hispanic didn't exist.

MCAD did respond to one element of the case where I stated I was bypassed for a training position in the academy by claiming that the city said I never applied for the position. I filed for an appeal and submitted an e-mail from LaVallee stating that I had applied for the academy position and that my training resume was requested. They city was caught in a lie, but by then it made no difference because the MCAD had already determined I was not a minority. My case was over. I started reading up on discrimination cases on my own and educated myself on the procedures. The police department and Davis never backed off with their unlawful discriminatory employment practices, and I was still within the time frame to file a fresh complaint. I did, but this time I acted as my own attorney.

I went right back to the MCAD office a month after it threw out my case and filed a new complaint in person. When I arrived, the MCAD staff clearly acknowledged that I was Hispanic and seemed puzzled as to why my original case was dismissed. When an attorney and a clerk pulled my dismissed case file, the clerk pointed out something on my file. The two women's faces immediately turned from a curious expression to an expression of acknowledgement with a head nod. They didn't share their knowledge with me, and I never found out what they saw in my file, but it was clear from their response that my case was unfairly dismissed.

I kept the case alive by submitting my own appeals after each attempt by the city lawyers to dismiss it. I attended dismissal hearings in person as my own attorney. This went on for some time, and I eventually reached the point where I needed a real lawyer again. I called approximately twenty lawyers trying to get someone to take on my case in a civil suit. At first, I couldn't get anyone to even listen to me. Sadly, discrimination cases can be hard to win and it takes a lot to get a lawyer to take one on. I finally called an office in Boston that agreed to meet with me.

Messing, Rudavsky, & Weliky only entertained serious clients, so to conduct an introductory meeting you were required to pay an attorney's fee for the time period of your interview. This law office had an excellent reputation in the area for cases like mine, so I agreed. I showed up with a briefcase of documents that supported my position.

I met with an attorney from the firm in a conference room, where he took on the position of the defense to disprove my case. At first, he was skeptical as he started firing a series of questions at me. Every time I answered, he asked, "Can you verify that?" I could, and for every answer I presented a document that authenticated my statement. Eventually his skepticism waned and he sat up straighter in his chair as he examined my documents carefully.

"Well, it appears you have substantial issues of workplace discrimination," he stated. "I'll have one of the partners examine your documentation and we will get back to you."

Once their firm wanted to take my case, I told them I may have difficulty securing the retainer fee and they then gave me the names of some attorneys that may take the case without such a high retainer. Suddenly it became much easier to get other lawyers to speak with me. When I called other law offices I would start the conversation with, "Hello, I was referred to your office by Messing, Rudavsky &

Weliky and I'm looking for assistance with an employment and discrimination case." Everyone was eager to speak to me now.

I interviewed a couple of attorneys, but when I met Marisa Campagna, she was authentically eager to take my case. After that, Marisa and I were pretty much in lockstep from beginning to end. My civil suit was filed in February 2003 and we spent the next three years working diligently to put the case together for trial.

Consistent Disparate Treatment

I transferred from the Waltham Police Department to Lowell in 1994. It came with a twenty thousand dollar a year increase in pay, and immediate reinstatement to the NEMLEC SWAT Team. It seemed like a good career choice. While in Waltham I had an assignment on the motorcycle unit, and actively instructed firearms for years. When I got to Lowell, they only had one firearms instructor for the whole department and he hadn't maintained his certification. Other than him, I was the only other qualified firearms instructor in the department at that time, so I was put to work conducting firearms training almost immediately.

Most of the weapons used by Lowell had been in service a long time and they looked it. Of a hundred fifty personnel, forty guys came to the range and had their weapons malfunction on the first or second round fired. It wasn't just because the pistols were old. I quickly learned that the officers in Lowell were told that lubrication was more important than cleaning the gun. Heavy lube in a dirty gun that sits in a holster for six months turns to grime, and this was the main culprit of the malfunctions. In the Marine Corps, the rule was that a clean gun is superior to a dirty, lubed gun. That's what I taught my platoon in the Corps and that's what I started teaching in LowelI. Proper cleaning and very light lubrication ended the malfunction issue.

Lowell still needed new guns, however. The department carried 9mm Beretta 92F's. I knew gun manufacturers often made good trade-in deals with police departments, and the .40 cal round was becoming popular because it had superior ballistics performance compared to the 9mm. I had contacted a representative at Beretta to negotiate a great deal for us to all get new .40 cal pistols at a trade in price between five and fifteen dollars a gun. The nomenclature of the two guns was the same, so it wouldn't require the additional familiarization training needed with a different gun. This would save the department thousands of dollars in training overtime.

I met with Davis to introduce my proposal and submitted the paperwork to support it. He flatly and immediately said it had no merit, and dismissed me. Approximately eight months later, it was announced in roll call that Timmy Crowley was working with Beretta to get the department new .40 cal pistols. Davis had given my proposal to Crowley to move ahead on and Crowley received the credit for the guns (Robert Alvarez v. City of Lowell, Jan. 11, 2006, P. 189). This is kind of a standard thing with cops, taking credit for another man's work. But I knew it had been my idea and my proposal, and I knew Davis knew it, too.

After I had been in Lowell for a little while, I learned we actually had a surplus of funds that were uncommitted. I suggested the Harley Davidson lease program may be a good use for them. Most police departments dedicate the motorcycle strictly to traffic enforcement, but with Lowell's topography, its dense population, and the myriad of tiny back streets and alleys; the use of motorcycles would give the department a clear edge getting into secluded places that were difficult to patrol in a cruiser. My suggestion was presented to Davis through my supervisor and he approved the lease program.

As the motorcycles became ready for delivery I ended up riding them all back to the station because of my past experience. There wasn't anyone else experienced riding a full-sized FLH. I wore my Waltham motorcycle uniform because no one had been fitted for motorcycle gear in Lowell yet.

As the motorcycle program was getting off, there was a vacancy in the housing unit where I worked, and where the motorcycle program was intended to be used. My supervisor approached me and asked if there was anyone in particular with whom I wanted to work. Scott Sauve and I worked together as Groton cops, so I suggested him, and he received the assignment. He and I attended the police motorcycle instructor course together.

During the instructor riding test, I missed a perfect score by one point and Sauve's score was one point above the failing score. It was good enough though, and Sauve and I became certified motorcycle instructors together. We began running two-week-long police motorcycle operator courses. After we certified Sergeant Russ Taylor, he approached me to write up an outline for the department's motorcycle policy. The original outline was adopted and used as the guidelines for the motorcycle program.

Tommy Kennedy was a student in one of the department's first motorcycle classes. On testing day at the end of two weeks of instruction, students need a minimum score of seventy to pass. Kennedy received a 43.

After we totaled his score, we told him he failed.

"What are you going to do about that?" he declared, petulantly.

I looked at him, bewildered for a moment before I realized what he meant. Apparently it was my responsibility to get him to pass. As instructors of the new program, we were under pressure to get all the Lowell cops certified, especially guys like Kennedy who were connected.

After thinking for a minute, I told him he could come back the following day to do over just the four exercises he failed. Actually, to retest, he should have had to complete the whole test with all the exercises, but we doubted his ability. If he failed to bring his score up I would have had to fail him. After retesting, we totaled his extra points. Redoing the exercises he initially failed brought his score up to a 70. He just made it. I hoped that after he gained more experience riding, he would improve. I was wrong.

When Davis removed me from the motorcycle unit, Sauve was the only other certified instructor. For the next three years of motorcycle classes, Davis appointed officers who were not certified instructors to take my place. This is the only time I ever heard of police training being conducted by people who were not actual instructors. Davis was so determined to keep me out, he put uncertified people in to teach with Suave instead.

At one point, Suave was suspended and Sergeant Taylor asked me if I could teach the school while he was gone. I naturally agreed; I wanted to teach again. It wasn't long before Davis found out and had me removed. He said he didn't want me teaching. He never gave a reason, he just didn't want it.

Years later, after Davis left for Boston, Lavallee became chief and eventually allowed me to return to motorcycle instruction. Each motorcycle class was two weeks long, but I was only allowed to teach for one week. Originally I thought it was Lavallee still playing games with me, but I learned that it was Sauve that had only scheduled me for the one week. He was titled the lead instructor of motorcycle training after I was removed, and I think he wanted to make sure he kept his title and position. Additionally, Crowley was now a lieutenant and was in charge of the motorcycles, and I'm sure Suave won some brownie points with him for this.

In 1996 and 1997, I started working as an executive protection detail leader for a company out of Boston. I was referred to the position by a close friend of mine, Walter Terzano. Walter and I served in the Marines together. I was a Platoon Sergeant, and he was a Marine in my platoon, so he had first-hand knowledge of my abilities as a leader and how I worked. Terzano was a private investigator for a company that mostly provided security overseas. They were looking to establish armed executive protection in the United States, but had not established stateside teams yet. My first job was to put together a team to provide security for a Jordanian businessman who would be traveling to Boston and New York. He had a high threat level in his home country and had his own armed security at home. The threat was low in America, but he wanted a skilled armed security detail in the United States anyway. He was pleased with the team I put together and the job went well.

The following year I was asked to come on board to supervise security for the CEO of a pharmaceutical company and his staff. They had received threats of harm from striking workers. I was number three in the chain of command, and as the job expanded we had approximately one hundred personnel providing security for the company in different facets. Ninety percent of the personnel were former Marines, Army Special Forces, SWAT officers, police officers, and state troopers.

In May 1997, I was informed that Internal Affairs had received a complaint that I was a supervisor of this security detail. The caller, who identified himself as Frank Shaw, said that I had a bad attitude and shouldn't have that level of responsibility. Frank Shaw was a retired Metropolitan District Commission (MDC) cop. He was given an administrative job next to my office and I worked closely with him. He never made that call. When I told him someone may want to interview him from my department's Internal Affairs, he was clearly upset and eager to clear his name and the accusations against me. Internal Affairs never contacted him or conducted an investigation. It based its conclusion on only the anonymous phone call. It was well known in the department that I was working security because I had asked a few guys if they wanted to work for me. There's no telling who actually made the call, but it didn't matter much because no one in the department seemed eager to investigate anyway.

A few days later, I received an official reprimand, stating that I needed to ask for permission before seeking outside employment, so I sent a request to Chief Davis. My request was denied and I was told that continuing to work would result in a suspension or termination. Davis claimed it was because someone told him that I planned to work in Lowell eventually and that was not allowed. There were no regulations in Lowell that prohibited security work, nothing I did in regards to this job went against department policy, no matter what Davis said. I was forced to leave my executive protection position, which was a loss of approximately $45,000 a year. This was shortly after Davis instructed his command staff to find any way to screw with me, six weeks after the Kennedy incident.

The reasons I was given for why I could not work as an independent contractor for an executive protection company that largely operated outside of Lowell clearly only applied to me. Approximately twenty percent of the officers in Lowell had outside employment and as far as I knew, none of them had requested permission. The only restriction was that officers could not own bars within the city limits, and that was a new policy that had just been implemented within the previous year or so. Several of the men owned construction companies. There were a few lawyers, including Tommy Kennedy, who worked in the same court that they also testified in as police officers, which clearly represents a potential conflict of interest. A couple of officers, including Buckley, opened their own executive protection company, and advertised inside of Lowell. Their company had a very short life span.

Keeping up with what was policy in the Lowell Police Department wasn't always easy. When officers were hired, we were given a manual that outlined the policies and procedures we were supposed to follow. This manual was extremely outdated, however. It was so outdated that it had a section detailing what types of work female officers were and were not allowed to do (Robert Alvarez v. City of Lowell, Jan. 25, 2006, P. 57), and different sections for males and females instructing us on how to wear our uniform. Female officers were only allowed to wear skirts by policy in the early days. Obviously these policies were no longer applicable in 1997, and so many of the rules had changed so often that the book was practically useless.

The manual did have a section on outside employment. One of the requirements of outside work when the manual was written was that the officer had to work in Lowell. The need to work within Lowell was no longer important once everyone had cell phones and could be quickly notified if there was an emergency and they were needed. Also, officers could not take a job that would prevent them from coming in as a police officer at any time if needed. There was nothing in the manual to suggest that the work I took on was inappropriate.

Whenever a change was made to the policies, it was usually given to us verbally during roll call. If it was an important change, it would be written out and we were all required to sign it to ensure it had been seen by everyone. Other times policies changed without notification. It was an inefficient system at best, and it was easy for an officer to miss a memo. Davis claimed he had issued the order that outside employment needed written permission, but that it had been a verbal order (Robert Alvarez v. City of Lowell, Jan. 25, 2006, P. 54).

When I filed my lawsuits against the department, for some reason Davis changed his position and allowed me to take on outside employment. By then it was too late. When I was forced to quit, I was quickly replaced. Although there were many people who knew me and were aware of my abilities, there were many who didn't, and Davis' stories of me being out of control and unstable had traveled throughout the law enforcement community. My outstanding reputation had been irreparably damaged by Davis' rants.

It wasn't until 2004, when Terzano was on his own and had secured a job protecting retired General Norman Schwarzkopf, that I was able to do executive protection work again. Terazano brought me on board the team and I served as tactical supervisor. We also provided security for Benjamin Netanyahu, the prior prime minister of Israel at the time, as a courtesy during an event at MIT in Boston. This was less than three years after 9/11 and the whole country was still on edge. There was absolutely no way we were going to allow anything to happen to these men. This was the last executive protection job I had.

Over the years, I came to the realization that my career was over and I was constantly looking for a way to leave the police department and move on to another job with equivalent pay. But what was there? I was a commercial diver in New York City before I became a cop, but I couldn't go back to that after twenty years. After 9/11 and the invasion of Iraq, guys with executive protection experience were landing six figure incomes overseas as military contractors. When Davis ended my executive protection supervisor job, I had no idea the repercussions would be so far reaching. If I had been allowed to continue, I would have had years of experience in the field and easily could have secured one of these jobs.

In 1998, I got the flu and called in sick for three days. Because Davis had instructed his staff to look for anything for which to discipline or suspend me, Captain Billy Taylor noticed that my sick days overlapped with sick days that Suave had taken. Once again, I was the topic of discussion at a command staff meeting. I was investigated for sick time abuse, in spite of the fact that I had accrued more sick days than most officers, and the last time I called in sick was with a life threatening injury three months earlier. I provided documentation of my illness, and was informed that the documentation might not be satisfactory. It was a ridiculous claim because I had several avenues available to me to take a few days off if I wanted to spend time with another officer and none of those avenues would have put my job at risk. Why would I call in sick to be with another cop? The investigation never went anywhere, but it was never closed either. I guess they were hoping for evidence to miraculously present itself. As I mentioned before, this is the Ed Davis hallmark technique of police investigation, accuse first and find evidence later, if at all.

I couldn't use sick time when I was sick and I couldn't use my vacation time. I was trapped in that shit hole. I was repeatedly denied specialty assignments for which I was qualified, vacation requests, and swap requests. Not being able to take a day off in three years was one of the hardest things to bear during these times. Constantly working in an environment where you know many of your coworker's hate you and your supervisors are always looking for ways to hurt you is fatiguing, to say the least. My work environment was so hostile that it was actually safer on the street than in the station. While it wasn't a guarantee that all vacation requests would be granted, I was denied every single time.

Before the Kennedy incident, I would go mountain climbing in the spring and the fall every year. I really missed it. You can only carry over a set amount of vacation days each year and because all requests to use vacation time were being denied, I lost some vacation days each year for three years in a row. Once I had Marisa as my attorney and the civil lawsuit was filed, my vacation requests finally began to be approved.

To Be a Detective

When I first got to Lowell, it quickly became clear to me that the department was run very differently than the departments where I had previously worked. I wouldn't describe it as a professional department at all. They appeared very loose with rules and regulations, and things were more crass and blunt. The lines seemed blurred. When I was in Waltham, you knew the department policies and it was clear what you could do and couldn't do. In Lowell, there was almost an anything goes mentality for the higher ups. The rules only applied to some of us.

I never saw how bad it was until after the incident with Tommy Kennedy. When I had a chance to step back and really look at my history with the Lowell Police Department, however, I realized that the roots of corruption and discrimination that Ed Davis built his empire on ran deep. At first glance, it wasn't noticeable. However, as I put all the pieces together the truth became glaringly obvious. The generally accepted mentality was that Irish guys made the best cops. Those who were not connected could find a place within the hierarchy as a minion if they acknowledged that as the truth, and only if they realized they could never rule. I didn't play their game; I didn't pander to their preconceived notions of who was better than whom. I was a peasant with royal aspirations and they didn't like that.

Outsiders from Lowell are called "blow ins," a derogatory comment used to separate the peasants from the royalty. I didn't realize I was a minority blow in, the worst kind of blow in there was. Minorities were inferior, but they "had" to hire them because of bureaucratic rules of discrimination. I don't know how often I heard someone say the quality of the police departments in the United States decreased when they had to hire all these minorities before they could hire white guys.

They all seemed to forget how they got hired because their father, brother, uncle, or cousin helped them get on. They never considered this to be an advantage. It was their job, their families' job. This was an exclusive club with a frat boy mentality and outsiders were not welcome. Moreover outsiders who refused to acknowledge these unwritten rules would be made to suffer.

If there was a discrepancy in their background, it could be forgiven or overlooked, while minorities, who were nobodies, would be quickly disqualified for the same things. For example, Kennedy failed his psychological screening in Nashua. If he wasn't white and connected, he never would have been hired in Lowell. There is evidence to suggest that there are other officers who were hired in Lowell because of their connections, in spite of the fact that they were obviously under-qualified.

In 1996, I interviewed for a detective position within the Criminal Investigations Bureau in Lowell. I had been an officer for nine years at that point and it appeared to be the natural next step in my career. I preferred making arrests and having court time over working traffic details, and one of the requirements for the position as it was posted was experience testifying in court. I had extensive experience on the stand over the years, and I averaged about eight hours testifying per month.

I was interviewed by Captain Billy Taylor, Deputy Chief Dennis Cormier, and Captain Bobby DeMoura. The interview started off fairly normal, with the expected questions about my work history and qualifications. When they asked about court experience they appeared put off that I had so much experience, but I didn't think much of it. Then, innocently enough, Taylor asked me about the future.

"Where do you want to go with the department?" he asked. "What are your plans?"

"Well, I'd like to be a detective a few years, and then I'd like to get promoted to Sergeant," I replied. This seemed like a reasonable answer; it was the truth and I assumed the goal of most competent police officers was to move up in the ranks throughout their career. But it was the wrong answer. They made it clear that they were not happy with my future plans at all.

"What the hell do you want that for? You don't want that!" Demoura snapped.

"That's really not for you!" Taylor chimed in.

This puzzled me. Why would they be angry at me for wanting a promotion, for wanting to be Sergeant? It appeared strange, and I didn't know what to think of it. Now I get it. They were looking at me like I was clearly below them. Not just in rank but as a person. Their preference was for Sergeant positions to go to their friends and family. I didn't belong there, I just got to work there. There was an element of nervousness, too, like they were almost scared that I might actually get promoted someday. Based on my experience, they didn't want me to be successful there because Lowell was a family-run police department that was always dominated by Irish families from Lowell and always would be.

I wouldn't be surprised to find out that they went back and told Davis what I said. He knew I had expectations to move up, and they all knew I was a professional. I tipped them off ahead of time that I had plans, and they were just waiting for the chance to shut me down and put me in my place. When I made Kennedy cry, they seized the opportunity to do so.

They gave the position I interviewed for to David Geoffroy, who is the nephew of Deputy Dennis Cormier, the same Cormier who interviewed me for the position. When I interviewed, I had nine years of police experience to Geoffroy's three years. I had seven commendations, and, to my knowledge, Geoffroy had none. I had nine years of extensive court experience with more than 200 hours of court testimony. This was a requirement sought after during the interview and it clearly exceeded Geoffroy's experience. I had a Master's Degree; Geoffroy had no college.

A few years later, in 1998, Geoffroy's paycheck stubs were found at a known drug dealer's residence during a drug raid, along with a police scanner that was tuned to a clandestine police radio frequency used exclusively by the Lowell Drug Unit. Officer Dave Pender was part of the raid team and reasonably suspected that Officer Geoffroy sold the secret police frequency to the dealers in exchange for drugs. Pender was told not to share this information with anyone. Geoffroy attended a drug abuse program and Davis removed him from the Criminal Bureau, but he did not receive any other discipline in response to his actions and no one ever threatened to fire him.

Steve Ciavolla is another example of someone who was made detective for reasons other than experience and ability. He was hired as an officer in the Lowell Police Department in November 1995, in spite of a criminal history and an active arrest warrant for probation violation (Chestnut). Ciavolla had friends in the department who undoubtedly assisted him in his efforts to get hired.

Ciavolla received assignments to specialty units that were out of reach for me. He later became a detective, and he is a good example of the type of person Davis wanted to have as a detective in the department. Ciavolla was a strong kid who knew how to fight. He was used as a "heavy hand" by officers of rank. He was a kid led down the wrong path from day one.

It wasn't long before civil lawsuits began to be filed against the city for police brutality where Ciavolla was the focus of the claim. During the lawsuits, all of Ciavolla's criminal history came out. His arrest records contained priors for assault and battery, shoplifting, and a being a minor in possession of alcohol. It's unknown how much the city actually paid out for these cases. He received a suspension but was never fired.

Even with his less than exemplary background, Ciavolla demonstrated more character than most of the command staff in my eyes. Lowell was a pretty violent place and some cops didn't show up to calls or waited until it was safe to show up. Ciavolla showed up. He was brutal, but I really don't frown upon being brutal when it's applied under appropriate circumstances. The last I heard of him, he was out on medical leave for stress.

As a police officer, it usually takes five years before you are not seen as a rookie anymore. Maybe this is a little different in an area with very high crime and a lot of action, but generally it takes about that long for an officer to go on enough calls to know how to handle a situation without any guidance or assistance from a supervisor. There is a level of skill involved: the ability to read people, comprehension of what you can and can't do, skillfulness in controlling a scene, knowledge of the law, and an understanding of how the court responds to different charges.

The detective position should be offered to capable officers who have gained the skills and abilities necessary to do well in that that role. Most departments promote seasoned officers to detective, where their experience and knowledge can be put to good use. Most departments truly want the best person for the job. This was not my experience in Lowell when I worked there, and as far as I know, not much has changed.

In Lowell, officers frequently made detective while they were in their first probationary year. It wasn't a role that you earned because of your knowledge and expertise; it was a gift that was given to officers who fell into place and did as they were told, a way to move up a little in the ranks if they weren't connected. One female officer with less than a year made detective after getting roughed up on a call one night. She wrote to Davis requesting a reassignment because she was uncomfortable working the street. Most of people who made detective knew they didn't really deserve to be there, thus they could be manipulated.

A newly minted detective could be asked to close out cases without a proper investigation to keep friends of the command staff out of trouble. They could be asked to sign the search warrant for cases on which they never worked. Officers who were competent and experienced were not wanted in the criminal bureau, because they couldn't be manipulated.

The public has the completely wrong idea from television of what a detective does. They're not the all-knowing seasoned veterans. They don't come onto the scene to collect clues and solve the crime while patrolmen stand around waiting to do their bidding, at least that's not what I experienced in Lowell. The only time I would call a detective is if I needed photos of a scene, or I if I needed them to collect evidence I couldn't. Usually I pointed out what I needed when he or she arrived. Often, detectives were called to a scene when there were too many witnesses or witnesses that needed a lengthy interview. If I didn't have enough information to take out charges, then detectives would follow up from the original report. There really wasn't any mystical skill involved, at least not from my experience in Lowell.

I would come to realize that not receiving the detective position would have a long reaching effect on my career goals, not just within Lowell, but elsewhere as well. In October 2007, I applied for a position with Military Professional Resources Inc., (MPRI). I was interested in the Law Enforcement Professional (LEP) program for law enforcement professionals to serve in Iraq and Afghanistan. A LEP would be embedded into a Marine or Army infantry unit in a forward area and utilize his police experience as an investigator and adviser. The requirements for this position specified individuals with experience investigating gangs, narcotics, violent crime, organized crime, and terrorism as well as being physically fit for harsh conditions. As I read the requirements, I felt confident that I had the necessary experience in all of these areas aside from organized crime and terrorism. However, it is rare that cops have any actual terrorism experience or are experienced with organized crime other than wiretaps, so I felt this would not affect me too negatively.

They also wanted someone with military experience. I joined the Marine Corps when I was seventeen and became a platoon sergeant of a surveillance and target acquisition (STA) platoon when I was 21. I submitted my military fitness reports, where my evaluations were listed as "outstanding" in overall performance, along with my initial application. Shortly thereafter, a recruiter from the company, who was also a prior Marine, contacted me. He concurred that I fit the requirements for the position and gave me the impression that I had a good chance of getting hired. I began to submit the additional documentation and medical records that were requested.

I started to get really excited that I would get the job and finally be able to leave the police department. No more being around cops, I'd be in theater with grunts instead. I wouldn't be owned by an enlistment. I'd be able to work independently outside the rank structure yet still provide service. It was a position where you could create your own value to the unit through hard work if you were committed and capable. Although you were incorporated into a team, it was a stand-alone performance job. You make it or break it on your own merit. It also paid around $230,000 annually.

This was my dream job. It seemed like the perfect fit for me. I wanted to wear a uniform with an American flag on the sleeve that stood for something again. I always held the flag as being something sacred to me. I wasn't from a police family where you can learn how to navigate all the secret privileges into which you were born.

When I was 10 months old, I became a foster child. I was taken in and raised by a working class, white family. This is the only family I ever knew and I was never treated like a foster child. My grandfather was a WWI veteran and my dad was a WWII and Korean War veteran. My brother did two tours in Vietnam, and was at Tan Son Nhut air base during the TET offensive in 1968.

I remember watching the news on TV with footage of the base being overrun during TET. It was horrifying for my parents and me to think we may be watching his death. We were a proud patriotic family in an era when it was more popular to burn the flag than salute it.

I embraced my American ethics and principles early on in life, and have tried to live by these standards to this day. I knew I was going to join the Marines when I was eight years old. I joined in 1976, a very unpopular time to be in the service. When I joined the police force, I genuinely thought my principles would be the foundation on which I could build my career. Truth, justice, fairness, integrity, credibility, courage, leadership, and humanity are just words thrown around to trump up the facade.

The flag on my police uniform was a mere decoration. In Lowell we didn't wear uniforms. We wore costumes by definition. We were all making believe we were something we were not. The badge, which is a distinct symbol of the police officer, sadly no longer held any significance to me. The badge should have exemplified these principles, but in Lowell these principles are all betrayed. To me, the American flag embodied the ethical symbol of our country as a whole and what we stand for as a people, not just a subset group. I am indignant that the Lowell Police uses the flag because in my opinion the department is a complete betrayal of any American principle.

My wife was totally supportive of the MPRI job. She knows what I'm about, and has been with me through all these events. When we discussed it, she said, "If you're going to die, I'd rather have you die among a bunch of Marines than to die on the streets of Lowell alone." Isn't she great? She's a true Spartan mother.

As I was moving through the hiring process, I received a phone call from my recruiter. He said his boss, who was prior FBI and ran the program, told him I didn't fit the requirements because I had never held the title of detective or investigator. The recruiter was still a supportive advocate and believed it was an uphill battle, and there was still a chance I could get the job.

Then I realized that one of the job's requirements was the ability to obtain a top secret security clearance, which would involve a thorough background investigation. They would be interviewing the police department command staff concerning their opinion of me. If my experience didn't speak for itself without a qualifying title, then I really didn't have a chance once the Kennedy incident and lawsuit came to light. Most likely they would receive a vilified interpretation from the police department. Even with a quality background investigation, an unbiased observer could deny the security clearance just as a precautionary measure. This, coupled with the head of the program doubting my qualifications, resulted in my decision to withdraw my application.

I was devastated. Even though the Kennedy incident and the suspension had happened so long ago, the ramifications of this injustice continued seriously to impact my life in such a detrimental way that I began to feel like I would never get away from it.

Awards

> The Lowell Police Department will award and honor those police employees whose actions are considered above and beyond the call of duty. Police personnel will be recognized for their achievements and rewarded justly by the issuance of specific enamel ribbon bars and/or medals (Operations Manual Order).

One of the primary arguments that Davis used as reasoning for removing me from all of my positions, including SWAT, was that I was mentally unstable and a danger to other police officers. He never made any attempt to have me examined psychologically, because he knew what the results would be.

Over the years, Davis repeatedly refused to issue awards that had been recommended by supervisors (Robert Alvarez v. City of Lowell, Jan. 25, 2006, P. 137). Awards would have been quickly issued if the acts were performed by anyone else. But Davis vehemently needed to demonstrate that his assessment of me as "a danger to other police officers" was a true and accurate statement. To support his executive assessment, he clearly could not issue me any award, especially the medal of valor. Any recognition of my conduct and performance would completely destroy his declaration of me. He could not and would not be proven wrong.

I personally couldn't give a damn about receiving an award issued by the likes of such a despicable character as Davis. What really irked me was the hypocrisy and Davis' blatant abuse of his authority for his own personal bigotry. I got satisfaction out of the knowledge that Davis would have to come face to face with his lie every time a recommendation for an award or a report of outstanding performance hit his desk. Although I knew he would always deny me any form of recognition for a job well done, I knew it pissed him off that I constantly proved him wrong again and again. His only response could be to delve deeper into his lie.

Davis issued an amendment to the manual that specifically outlined what the requirements were for certain awards, to enable officers to know when they should be nominated for an award and what the criteria were. However, just doing something that met the requirements was not enough to earn an award. Like everything else in the department, award issuance usually had a political flair associated with it.

In September 1999, I was sent to break up a party that had gotten out of control. I arrived to find what looked like a house full of minors in full swing, drinking and doing who knows what else. In most police departments, they would assign at least two units for a call like this, but not in Lowell. For a number of the years I worked there, I handled most of my calls alone. Sometimes a second unit was assigned, but in a lot of cases they showed up after the arrest was made and the event was over, if at all. Dispatchers, street sergeants, and everyone else knew that there were certain people who didn't have to answer the radio, or who were allowed to get away with responding to calls for service by just saying they were tied up.

The backup situation changed from year to year when we received new assignments. There were good cops working the street that would come out of the woodwork to help but it seemed I usually had a guy in the next sector over who just didn't show. There were a few years that I worked a two man car and rode with decent guys, but in my last several years I worked alone. After 2006, the department hired a number of veterans and they were all good kids; a breath of fresh air that made my last few years on the force tolerable.

When I saw how big the party was, I called in to report what I had and to say that I needed some assistance. As dispatch called around to see if someone was free to assist, I went inside. I didn't bother to wait for backup because I didn't think anyone would actually show. To be completely honest, I actually felt safer by myself. I didn't have confidence in a lot of other cops in the department at the time.

Most of the kids at the party were about twenty years old, but there were a few who were younger, some as young as thirteen or fourteen. There were also several known Asian gang members present. There had just been a shooting by a rival gang a few days earlier, which always meant there would soon be other shootings throughout the city in retaliation. This made the situation much more intense than it may have been otherwise because I knew some of these guys may be armed.

I worked to get everyone escorted out of the house, standing in a narrow hallway as kids squeezed past me. Most of them shuffled past with their eyes averted, hoping to avoid trouble. Then I felt this one kid lock his eyes on me. His right hand was tightly shoved into his jacket pocket, and it keyed up my awareness level. I instinctively reached out and grabbed his right hand with my left hand. I took a quick breath; I had just grabbed a gun that was pointed directly at me.

I felt the hard steel through his jacket, and I realized I held onto a snub nosed revolver and that I had my hand around the cylinder. I held on tight, knowing that the gun was disabled. As long as I held the cylinder, he couldn't pull the trigger. I threw a right punch to his chest. His feet flew off the ground and he slammed into the wall across from me as the adrenaline that was suddenly coursing through my veins caused me to use a bit more force than I realized. He landed back on the floor and curled over for a moment, gasping.

I had a moment to get a better look at him; he was small and probably only weighed about 120 pounds. As I started to process this, I felt a tug on the jacket and looked down to see him struggling to slip out of it. He was trying to get away! Unfortunately for him, I had a death grip on the gun and his arm was twisted in the sleeve. It slowed him down just enough. I tackled him and was putting cuffs on him as backup stormed in.

I always wore a ballistic vest from the first day on the job to my last, but if he fired and caught me low, just under the vest, I probably could have died there on that filthy hall floor that night. If I had, he most likely would have never been caught because I was alone. Backup didn't arrive until I knelt on this kid's back to handcuff him. At the booking window we found out that he was only fourteen and that his older brother who was eighteen was already doing time in jail for murder.

By order of Chief Davis himself, the Medal of Valor "shall be awarded to Lowell Police Officers who effect of attempt the arrest of a dangerous felon in the commission or attempted commission of a crime, and placing the officer in danger of his/her personal safety (Operations Manual Order)." It is also given when the actions of the officer save or attempt to save another person's life. It is the second highest award a Lowell Police Officer can receive.

This event and arrest clearly surpassed any previous issuance of the Medal of Valor. Leavitt and Crawford received the Medal of Valor for the felony car stop I supervised during the Kennedy incident. Another officer received the Medal of Valor for being in a foot pursuit of a suspect who threw a gun away while being chased. None of these guys had a suspect holding a loaded weapon pointed at them while they made an arrest.

In March 1999, I responded to a call of multiple gunshots in a densely populated neighborhood. When I arrived, I found twelve warm, spent, brass cartridges on the ground. They were 7.62 X.39 cartridges which I knew came from either an SKS or an AK-47 assault rifle. There were several bullets holes in three homes across from the parking lot. With all that rapid gunfire, no one ventured to look outside to see what was happening. Normally when there was a shooting like this, on-call detectives from the day shift would have been paged and sent out, but with no witnesses and nothing other than the brass on the ground as evidence, there wasn't anything for them to do.

I could have just left it like this and written it up as is, but I started knocking on doors instead. Several people said they saw nothing, but I kept trying. I knocked on the door of a third floor apartment as a last resort. The door opened, and a young girl stood in front of me.

"Hi, I'm investigating the gunshots that went off earlier. Did you see anything at all by any chance?"

"No," she said. "No, I didn't see any of it. I just heard it."

"Ok, have you been outside at all tonight? Can you tell when you came home this evening?"

"Nope, been home all night, never went outside."

"Ok, had you looked outside at all? Like before or after the shooting?"

"I looked out after the shooting and saw nothing."

"Ok, how about before the shooting?"

"Ya, I looked out the window a while ago." She looked down at the floor for a second like she was thinking and then she looked back up at me. "Before it happened. There was a Ford Explorer out there with its lights on in the parking lot."

She directed me toward her window as she pointed. She pointed directly where I found the spent brass.

"Did you recognize the SUV or the driver?"

"No," she said.

"Is there anything about the SUV that you can remember? I really need some help here."

She looked down again for a second before continuing. "I did recognize the girl in the back seat. At least I think I did. I don't know her but I think she's going out with a guy who lives a couple of blocks down."

She directed me to an apartment building about half a mile away. As I was heading to the apartment, Jimmy Hodgedin showed up at the scene. He was a detective on the early night shift, and he came over just to check things out. I told him what I had and that I was going to check for the boyfriend. He and I headed over to the apartment building, which we knew was a real rat hole.

When we got to the apartment we met Sergeant Brendan Durkin, who heard we were trying to locate a suspect or witness from the shooting. My shift had already ended and Sergeant Durkin was a late night boss who had just started his shift. He had been a detective for years and was now back on patrol. Unlike most of Lowell's detectives, Durkin was actually skillful and capable. The apartment building was locked up and no one answered any of the door buzzers. Eventually, I climbed up the side of the building to an unlocked hallway window. After knocking on a few doors, we found the boyfriend. At first he wouldn't tell us anything, but we kept pushing him.

"Look, we're just looking to locate the girl you're seeing. That's all. Help us out and we'll be out of here." Eventually he gave us the name of his girl and where she lived.

Durkin and I headed to the girl's house and spoke with her and her parents. Durkin questioned her and she folded pretty quickly.

"Yeah, I was there. I was in the back seat of the truck, just along for the drive. Johnny (name changed) deals weed and he lives in Tewksbury. He's not a bad kid, he just deals in herb, that's all, you know?" She paused for a second, trying to decide how much to tell us.

"Look, he was going to make a quick deal for $500 worth of weed. He said he was sick and tired of getting ripped off when he made deals in Lowell, so he brought some kind of big ass gun. It freaked me out when he started waving it around, but I needed a ride. What was I supposed to do?"

I sketched a picture of an AK-47 on a piece of paper.

"Did it look like this?"

"Ya, that's the gun."

She paused again, nervous. "We sat in the parking lot for a bit. Then some black guy showed up and stood at the driver's door talking about the deal. He said he wanted to see the weed before he pulled his cash, but when Johnny showed it to him, he reached in and grabbed it and ran like hell. The next thing I know Johnny jumped out of the truck and started shooting at the guy but he got away. I can give you his address, just don't tell him it was me, okay?"

With the shooter's name and address we met with the Tewksbury police department and called out the SWAT Team. We set up at the dealer's house, and a Tewksbury detective put a phone call into the residence and got the guy on the phone. Once he knew we had him cold, he surrendered to us without incident.

"With your rights in mind, where's the rifle?" I asked him.

"It's in the trunk right here."

I opened the trunk and found the AK-47 wrapped in a blanket. I logged the rifle into evidence, finished the report, and headed home at about 9:00 in the morning.

At the following command staff meeting, Davis was forced to admit that this was good police work, but no commendation was recommended. In the past, detectives who staked out an escaped convict's home made a warrant arrest when the guy came home. They received a commendation for this miraculous feat.

In March 2000, I received a call for assistance in the foot pursuit of an assault and battery with a dangerous weapon suspect. The suspect was a kid who had beat a guy's head in with a rock during a failed drug deal. This was right at commuter time and the downtown area was strangled in gridlock. I saw a guy fitting the description walking down the sidewalk. I pulled up and had him at the right fender of the cruiser.

"Hey what's up? Can I talk to you for a second?" I asked as I got out of the car.

The kid immediately bolted. Normally I would have used the cruiser to chase him, but there was too much traffic and I had to chase him on foot. After getting around the cruiser the kid had a good jump on me, and I'd have to make up some distance. He was 21 in sneakers and shorts, and I was 43 with almost 30 pounds of gear on. We were still at a full sprint at about 100 yards when I managed to grab the back of his shirt. I was forcing him into the back of a parked car, hoping I could "check him into the boards," so to speak, but he fell down just before the car.

As he fell, I didn't let him go, which was a huge mistake. The back of the car came up fast and I thought I could get my hand up in time to block the hit but I was wrong. My chin hit the trunk right where the key goes in. All of a sudden my face was wet and there was blood everywhere. The pain was pretty intense but my personal rage trumped any pain. The kid was still on the ground as I got up, and I immediately jumped on him. As I knelt on his back, blood was pouring out of my mouth and hitting him in the face and the ground in front of him.

"I'm hurt!" he screamed. "I'm bleeding...I'm bleeding!"

"Shut up asshole," I said as I handcuffed him. "That's my blood. Stop being a pussy."

When I looked at the car, there was a good sized dent where my jaw hit, and an imprint of my badge was embedded in the trunk. I could feel a bunch of teeth missing, but I couldn't find them. I had guys look under the car and on the hood, but they were nowhere to be found.

The doctors found my teeth at the hospital. Four of them had snapped off and were embedded in my mangled lower lip. My head had snapped back and caused a cervical and spinal compression. I was out of work for nine months and had approximately 40 hours of dental work done.

Previously, officers were working a festival where livestock was on display when a bull escaped and ran down the street. An officer chased the bull and the bull turned on him and gored him in the leg. The officer received a pretty severe wound that put him out of work for a couple of years. There was a female officer present who attempted to shoot the bull with her 9mm pistol (Robert Alvarez v.

City of Lowell, Jan. 26, 2006, P. 88-89). Her rounds were found to have hit vehicles parked in the area. When the bull turned toward her, she jumped into a nearby motorist's car. There, in a panic, she accidently fired rounds into the dashboard of the car. The shooting stopped when she attempted to reload her pistol by inserting a magazine backwards into the gun. Davis issued the medal of valor to both officers.

In December 2004, a mother called 911 because her three year old son was choking on something and not breathing (Holland). Officer Ung was dispatched to the call along with the fire department and I was assigned as backup. Like the Kennedy incident, I was pretty far away and I arrived last. I pulled up behind the fire truck.

As I exited the cruiser, it was dark and cold and all I could hear was screaming. I headed to where I heard the screaming coming from, and I saw this little boy face down on the lawn in a puddle. Ung stood in the driveway looking helpless as the parents of the boy screamed.

"He's choked on something!" someone said to me. "He's been down for a while."

I looked over to Officer Ung, pissed and puzzled.

"I've done back lowers, but I can't get anything. I'm not getting any response," he shrugged.

"Why the hell is he lying in a puddle?" I asked, enraged.

I knelt in the puddle and flipped the boy over. He was light blue and he had no pulse; he wasn't breathing at all. I've seen dead children before and my heart sank. All I could think was that this kid was dead. I immediately opened his airway and started doing chest compressions, but I had little hope. I did this for about a minute when his eyes rolled back in his head and his arm flipped. I heard him start breathing, and he came back; he had a pulse.

I was completely shocked and thrilled at the same time. I don't think I ever felt like that before. I went from complete despair to total joy. I had done CPR before, and most people don't make it. It was amazing that this little boy would now have his life back and his parents wouldn't be burdened with all that sorrow.

My facial expression never changed, this was a completely personal and internal thing. Davis and the others would later testify that I was always mad and stone-faced. I never allowed others to see how I was feeling while I worked in Lowell because I never felt like it was safe to do so, even during this episode, which was one of the most amazing moments of my life.

Just as the boy started to breathe, the EMTs showed up and I gave care of the child over to them. The boy had swallowed a fireball, and the EMTs were able to dislodge it. It was right around Christmas time, and he got into some candy by himself in the kitchen. It blocked off his airway and was the reason why he stopped breathing and his heart stopped. He was transported to the hospital where he was listed in urgent but stable condition. A few days later it was reported that he had made a full recovery with no brain damage.

This incident was reported in the newspaper and subsequently both Ung and I received the lifesaving award. Davis would have been hard pressed not to issue an award due to the media involvement, especially because my civil lawsuit against the department for discrimination was pending when this occurred. I'm sure he was under pressure and felt he could not freely express his bigotry.

Officer Ung was hired in 1992, and was the first Cambodian officer to be hired on the department. Because of the huge Cambodian population in Lowell, the department was under pressure to hire Cambodians so that the police force reflected the community better. Ung spoke with a heavy accent and had average-to-poor writing skills. Overall, my experience was that he was despised by most of the other cops because they had to hire him over a white guy. Ung served as a Khmer interpreter for the department, and had served as an interpreter for the DEA, FBI, and Secret Service.

In 1993, Ung was reprimanded for brandishing his service weapon in public on two occasions. They tried to fire Ung at this point, but were unable to get any of the Cambodian people present to bear witness against him. Later he was suspended for violating the grounds of his reprimand. In 2004, he was finally fired for filing false police reports. He towed a woman's car to get back at her for money that she owed him.

I would like to compare the careers of Ung and Kennedy while they worked for the Lowell Police Department. Both officers were small and physically weak and their performance can be described as equally abysmal. Ung clearly did not have the necessary attributes to be a police officer, much like Kennedy. It was apparent to me that both men became officers for reasons other than skill and ability. Yet their careers took two completely different trajectories. Ung received discipline several times and was eventually fired. Kennedy's career should have followed the same path, but he was always taken care of. The higher ups covered for him and enabled him to be promoted to captain and ultimately sixth in line for chief of police. His rise in the ranks in Lowell was actually described as "meteoric" in my case. The only differences between the two men was their race, and Kennedy's connections. Kennedy was royalty and Ung was a peasant. This is how these Irish police families maintain control and perpetuate the lineage of corruption.

During my career, I had a number of run-ins with suicidal people. One shift during the summer, when it was around 100 degrees, I was partnered with Chris Hanson and we received a call for a suicidal female. Upon arriving at her apartment, I knocked on the door. It swung open, and before me was a five foot nine, two-hundred pound, naked woman with a foot long butcher knife in her hand.

"I'm going to die and you're going to watch me," she gasped hysterically.

I stepped back from her to discretely draw my weapon and held it low as I maintained eye contact. I learned over the years that the best approach in these situations is to speak in a casual manner as if it's no big deal, in order to drop the drama level down.

"Ok, what's your name?" I asked.

"Mary," she said, looking at me distrustfully.

"Ok, Mary, I know you want to die. Can you tell me why?"

I knew I was taking a chance with this. Sometimes having people talk and vent is helpful but sometimes recalling the traumatic, painful event can throw them over the edge. It was a gamble, but a method that I learned was effective if it worked. I've seen cops say, "You don't want to do that. You don't want to die," to suicidal people, but I have found that's the wrong thing to say. I don't tell them how they should feel. Clearly, at that moment they want to die. That's how they feel. It's a fact that is real for them, don't deny that fact. It's the whole reason we're all standing there together at that moment in time.

She took a breath and then moved back into the apartment, still gripping the knife fiercely. I stepped across the apartment threshold, keeping her in sight.

"My life sucks," she said.

"I know. Life sucks a lot of the time, but can you tell me what's so bad today?" I asked.

She started hyperventilating and struggled to catch her breath. After what felt like a really long time, she finally sat down on the edge of the bed. She still held the knife tightly in her left hand. I stood in the corner of the room in case she decided to lunge at me.

"You must be getting tired holding that knife like that," I suggested gently.

She nodded and went to switch the knife to her right hand. When she did, I saw my opportunity to disarm her. I used an Aikido wrist lock as I grabbed her wrist, twisted it, and pulled the knife out of her hand. After that she just collapsed and went with the EMTs to the hospital without incident. When this happened, Jack Davis was a sergeant and had been my direct supervisor for six years. He put me in for an award for this incident, but his brother denied it as usual.

Another time, Officer Louie Rios was on foot patrol when a passing motorist told him that they believed that a man was about to jump off the overpass on Middlesex Street. He radioed it in and I happened to be nearby. As I came to the overpass, Rios was approaching the man, who was on the other side of the bridge. He was facing out away from the bridge, with his hands behind him, and he was leaning forward.

I exited the cruiser and Officer Rios and I ran up to him because he looked like he was going to jump. He saw us approaching and he let go just as we got there. We grabbed him by his arms just as he let go. He was pretty light, about 120 pounds. We pulled him up and flipped him in the air because he was so small, and we pulled him back over the railing. We were put in for an award, but again received nothing.

In November 2007, after my case was concluded, I was called to back up Jimmy Matos with a suicidal male. We entered the front door and found an elderly couple in their pajamas sitting and calmly watching "Wheel of Fortune." They had called us, but it appeared as though we were disturbing them. They were more focused on solving the puzzle than they were on telling us what was going on. They nonchalantly explained that their son was in the bathroom with a knife, wanting again to kill himself. The father pointed down the hall toward the back of the house where the kitchen was.

"The bathroom is right off the kitchen," he said, never taking his eyes off the television screen. We headed down the hall, not alert to the level we should have been. I arrived ready for anything, because it was a man-with-a-knife-call, but I let it ease after speaking with the serene, pajama-wearing parents. We stood in front of the bathroom door and asked the son to please step out.

"Fuck you, leave me alone," he shouted through the door.

Matos looked at me and I nodded. He opened the bathroom door and we immediately saw this guy bleeding profusely from both arms. He held a bloody ten inch butcher knife at shoulder height, ready to attack us. In half a heartbeat we drew our guns.

"Drop the knife!" we both yelled, simultaneously.

"Fuck you, shoot me!" he yelled as he lunged at Matos, attempting to stab him. Jimmy moved back and got out of range just in time. At that moment, we both had a clean close up shot at him, but neither of us took it.

He continued to lunge at us. "Fuck you. Shoot me! Shoot me! I don't fuckin' care!"

The fight moved into the kitchen and I grabbed a kitchen chair, holding it like a lion tamer while still covering him with my gun. He kept going after us with the knife. First to Matos, then me, then Matos. While I had him at bay with the chair, Jimmy gave him a good dose of OC pepper spray, hoping to disable him. It didn't work, and he maintained his stance. Matos then gave him a straight front kick that set him back a bit.

A half second later, Matos picked up a wooden kitchen gate. He threw it and hit him right in the face. This threw him off and Matos sprayed him again. I noticed Matos was fighting with two hands and had holstered his gun. This alarmed me, as I immediately became aware that I would have to shoot this guy if he lunged at Jimmy again because he was already in stabbing range. Matos threw another front kick with his size 13 shoe and hit the guy's knife hand. The knife sprung out of his hand and flew right up over our heads.

I think the three of us were all totally shocked because it was such a picture perfect move, but we didn't miss a beat because we were still fighting him. Once we got the guy down on the floor, he went totally berserk. I holstered my gun and we started to fight him with empty hands. We grappled on the floor for about a minute and finally managed to handcuff the guy. Matos and I started coughing hard because there was so much OC spray in the air that the kitchen was fogged. I looked around and saw that the kitchen was totally destroyed from our fight. Even after he was handcuffed, the guy continued to kick and scream the entire time. The EMTs came and took him out tied to a stretcher with the Hannibal Lecter mask to keep him from biting. He was taken to the hospital, where he was treated for psychiatric issues.

Afterwards, the whole incident was settling in on Jimmy. He had three years on the job at the time and I was one of his training officers when he first hit the street. This was his first deadly force fight.

"Why didn't we just shoot him?" he asked me.

"Because this guy had no real fighting skill and really didn't know how to fight with a knife. He was an emotional wreck." I said.

Jimmy paused for a moment, thinking about what I said. "Yeah, I guess you're right. How come this shit doesn't affect you?"

"I don't know. I been doing this for twenty years, and this was my third knife fight. I guess you just get used to it after a while."

Our supervisor submitted an award recommendation for us, saying that we showed great restraint in a deadly force scenario that was probably a planned intentional suicide by cop situation. He commended us for utilizing force techniques that used less levels of force than what is recommended. We saved this guy's life, and our actions resulted into a greatly de-escalated incident. Davis had gone to Boston at this point and LaVallee was now the chief. But LaVallee was another command staff officer who was less than honest under oath against me; he was part of Davis' camp. No award was issued to either of us.

Along with my lawsuit against the city, I always documented every incident of discrimination and disparate treatment that I encountered. I submitted these reports to Davis or his staff so they couldn't use the excuse of "I didn't know that" when we were in court. At some point, Davis created an awards committee of three command staff personnel. This committee was similar to Larry Hickman being the minority contact officer, useless. I sent a report to them questioning why awards were not issued for incidents I had been involved in when the criteria for awards had been met and recommendations had been submitted by my supervisors. The committee never responded. Like all the reports I sent to Davis requesting an explanation for his actions, I never received a response. I was a danger to other officers, and mentally unstable with a bad attitude, and that was that.

Where did all the money go?

Before I started working in Lowell, the department was struggling with a severe budget crisis. It needed to bring in a lot of money fast, or it would have to lay off a bunch of cops. Faced with the grim prospect of laying off a significant portion of his force, Chief Jack Sheehan asked Davis to apply for grants to help the department with its budget crisis. As Davis started doing research, he realized that most of the grants available would only be awarded to departments that were making a serious effort to adopt community policing measures.

He pointed this out to the city, and even though Sheehan was not entirely on board with the plan, everyone else was (Thacher), and Davis was given free rein to restructure the department as he saw fit in order to continue bringing money in. The city started to work toward moving Sheehan out of the way to allow Davis to become the new chief.

Davis applied for and received several grants for community policing, bringing a ton of money into the city to revive the police force (Thacher). The budget crisis was over, and the department hired 100 new police officers. Davis claimed that he used the money to establish community policing programs in Lowell, and dubbed himself the "godfather of community policing." He gained a lot of notoriety for the work he supposedly did, but community policing in action was not what he made it out to be.

One aspect of the community policing model involves addressing the fear of crime in the community. This became Davis' primary focus in his implementation of community policing principles in Lowell, and officers received assignments designed to reduce the appearance of crime often. He didn't seem to care much about properly reducing actual crime at all, instead his focus was on helping the citizens to feel good about the work he was doing.

Another aspect of the community policing model is the idea that officers should be involved in the communities with which they work, that knowing the citizens and having personal relationships allows an officer to have a better idea of where the crime is. Officers are encouraged to play basketball and become friendly with people in the neighborhoods where they work, to ensure the people of the community "feel good" about the work they are doing.

Davis implemented this idea in Lowell by working with members of the community to organize monthly meetings across the city. Sector captains were required to attend and participate in these meetings in order to find out what the local citizens were most concerned about, and the rest of us were encouraged to attend. In practice, it was the other way around mostly, where an officer assigned to an area would attend, and it was my experience that captains frequently didn't show up.

I attended a number of community meetings myself, and I found it was mostly citizens who weren't really dealing with real crime on a day-to-day basis. There were a lot of complaints about where neighbors placed their garbage cans, and the number of Asians moving into the area. These community meetings never produced any real intelligence on crime, and sometimes they produced false intelligence that wasted valuable resources. For example, one neighbor would accuse another residence of being a drug house because they were angry with whoever lived there. We would check out the story and find absolutely no drug activity. Addressing these issues decreased the "fear of crime" in the community, and appeased the concerns of the voting public, but it never made any difference with the actual crime that was occurring in Lowell.

I got better information when I spent as much time as possible on the street, interacting with people in high-crime areas, daily reviewing all recent arrest reports, and observing the activity in those areas in order to develop good crime intelligence. An essential source of intelligence was from prostitutes. These girls were addicts and at the bottom of the food chain, but they knew everything that was going on in the street. A five-minute conversation with a prostitute would yield more actionable intelligence than two months of community meetings.

Once, my sector captain came back from a community meeting and told me that the citizens there had expressed concern over activity that they had noticed in a neighborhood park. I already knew that the park was becoming a hotspot for crime, and I had been patrolling it for a few weeks. I informed him that I had already made a few arrests there, and that I was aware of what was happening. I knew what was going on in the community before my supervisors did, and I was already taking care of it. When this happened, the captain could attend the next meeting and announce that we had already been dealing with the problem.

One principle of my personal work ethic is not only to know my job, but to also know my boss' job. When the boss comes to you with questions and tasks, it's important to know the answer before the question. I always tried to do my job to the level where my boss didn't have to do his job. If your boss is confident in your skill and ability, he can sit back and you'll be left alone. When I was left alone to do my job, I could actually accomplish some of the community's needs before anyone else realized there was a problem.

Davis often wasted valuable resources on minor police issues in order to make the department look good to outsiders. For example, there was a woman who ran the Lower Highlands community meetings who was very vocal about how there were too many Asians moving into the area. Admittedly, there had been an increase in crime in her neighborhood because we had a lot of issues with Asian gangs in Lowell. We were fully aware of this, and because Asian families now occupied several tenement buildings near her, we patrolled the area regularly. We increased patrols in response to her complaints, but we couldn't evict people just because they were Asian. It still wasn't enough, and her complaints continued.

Davis responded to her complaints by having an officer sit in front of her house all day, every day, for two months. I was one of the men assigned to this role, and I spent my entire shift for two months sitting in a cruiser in front of her house and basically working as her private security guard. Naturally, she sang Davis' praises after that and she became his main cheerleader in the media. She was frequently quoted in the *Lowell Sun*, expressing what a great job Davis was doing.

Davis received a report once from a woman who wrote grants for the department that a payphone on Lower Middlesex Street was being used to make drug deals. This was in 1995, before cell phones, and there were a lot of rooming houses in the area. It was the only phone to which a lot of the people living in the rooms had access. There was naturally a lot of traffic coming and going because of this. The people using the phone were mostly poor, and that didn't "look good," which prompted the complaint. Any cop who worked the area knew this. We informed our supervisors of the situation, but the word came down that Davis wanted the telephones guarded by an officer around the clock.

I was one of the officers who received this assignment to stand by the pay phone. I had to spend my entire shift standing by this phone and telling people that they couldn't use it. If they complained, I directed them to another payphone several blocks away. I wasn't even allowed to take a break for dinner, someone brought me a sandwich that I ate standing up. I was assigned this post for a couple of weeks until Davis decided that the problem had been resolved and I was allowed to return to patrol duty.

Davis had no problem assigning officers to all kinds of static stationary posts, including providing security for himself. I once got called to watch his parked car for almost three hours while he took a woman out to dinner. I had to just stand there next to his car. What a waste of time. Other officers were often assigned to similar static details as well.

Davis left Lowell in 2006, but his influence can still be found there today. As of 2016, the Lowell, Massachusetts city website has a section on the methods employed by the police force there, based on community policing principles. It's a nice theory, however, in practice it doesn't really describe how the Lowell Police Department works.

The website states that "police are concerned not only with high-visibility crimes, but with minor offenses which contribute to fear of crime, and negatively effects public perception of city or neighborhood safety." Minor offenses were such as people living in rooming houses, using only one payphone.

It also says that "officers are given broad discretion to manage their own uncommitted time." This statement suggests that officers in Lowell are given a lot of latitude to determine where their work will be most effective in their designated geographical areas.

However, this is not the case in practice; instead, officers were often assigned to stay in one place for hours, doing what Chief Davis thought would be best. Having broad discretion to manage our own time rarely happened in spite of the fact the officers on the street knew our community best.

Additionally, the website says that the "police define success and accomplishment primarily by the results achieved and the satisfaction of the consumer of services, rather than by strictly internal measures of the amount of work completed." For example, when a personal security detail is placed in front of a woman's house for weeks and she then goes around talking about how wonderful the police force is, that is a greater measurement of success and accomplishment than using that time to arrest someone with an AK-47 who is planning to shoot up a neighborhood. Customer satisfaction above all else is an important goal for someone in sales; but as a police officer, sometimes other things should be a priority.

When Bill Clinton was President of the United States, he embraced the community policing model with open arms. He sponsored a set of bills that provided grants to police departments across the country that wanted to develop community policing programs of their own. These bills created the COPS program, from which most of the grant money came. COPS awarded grants to Lowell almost every year while Davis was Chief, and these grants were all designated as money to be used for the implementation of specific programs or training.

> "The COPS Office awards grants to hire community policing professionals, develop and test innovative policing strategies, and provide training and technical assistance to

> community members, local government leaders, and all levels of law enforcement. Since 1994, the COPS Office has invested more than $14 billion to help advance community policing." (United States Department of Justice)

Unfortunately, some of the cities that received the highest awards turned out to be rife with corruption. While some departments appeared genuinely to believe in the community policing model, others have suffered from bad national publicity due to police brutality issues, and many continue to hire officers who have been fired or turned away from other departments (Moraff). It appears as though Lowell is just one of a long list of cities that suffers from corruption and severe discriminatory practices.

So where did all the money go? Between 1993 and 1999, Ed Davis brought $12.4 million into Lowell as the result of his grant writing efforts. In 2001, COPS had invested over $5.6 million into programs for Lowell (Congressman Martin Meehan). That is a lot of money for a small city like Lowell. Davis made it appear as though the money went toward new and innovative community policing programs. Maybe some of it did. My experience was that most of the 'community policing' programs were a sham, however. The multi-million dollar question is, did they really spend all that money the way it was supposed to be spent?

It's difficult to pin down where all the money was spent because no one has access to Davis' records from the time. Based on what I have experienced with Davis, I wouldn't be surprised to find out they were all destroyed. There is ample evidence that the funds coming into Lowell were mismanaged, as well as evidence of employees stealing from the department. I don't have any hard proof that Davis and his cronies spent the grant money and other Lowell funds on things other than approved expenses. I do have examples that provide a reasonable doubt that all of the funds were disbursed appropriately. I will present the evidence I have, and that, coupled with the other information presented in this book, will hopefully show there is a strong probability that it didn't all go where it was supposed to go.

In 2000, Lowell was awarded $178,700 to create programs to "identify police practices and reforms to build trust, reduce police misconduct, and enhance police integrity" (Unknown, 2000). The city received $175,000 for the Weed and Seed program, and another $225,000 for the same program the following year (Congressman Martin Meehan). COPS invested a lot of money into Lowell to enhance police integrity, but it certainly wasn't spent on that. The officers in Lowell blatantly lied in court a number of times, both in my case and in other cases levied against the city. No efforts were genuinely made by Ed Davis to reduce police misconduct or enhance police integrity, ever.

One year, Lowell received a half of a million dollars from the COPS program to be used specifically for training on racial profiling and police integrity. I never participated in any training programs like this, so Davis obviously never followed through on it. With the amount of lying and racism that existed in the department when I worked there, it would have been money well spent; but racial profiling and integrity were definitely low priorities for Davis and his crew.

Departments that receive grants from COPS are subjected to audits to ensure they are using the funds properly. One appendix on the COPS website has Lowell listed as one of the worst cities on the medium grantees list for that year (Office of the Inspector General). Unfortunately, the year is not listed on the report, but of the 33 cities audited that year, only two scored worse than Lowell. An audit from 2005 that reviewed Lowell from 2000 to 2004 found a number of problems with the reporting and accounting measures used in Lowell during that time (Office of the Inspector General, 2005).

If Lowell was not meeting the reporting and accounting standards of the COPS program, and it was given grant money to create programs that were never created, wouldn't it make sense to believe that money was being spent elsewhere? On what did Davis spend all that money? Next we will look at some instances where money was definitely misappropriated.

A woman named Debra Coan worked in the payroll department. She was a civilian, and she had some very close friendships with a number of officers in the department. It was rumored by command staff that she would alter the timesheets after Davis signed off on them so her friends could get extra hours of overtime. Who knows how many thousands of dollars she cost the department.

Coan also worked at Filene's in the Nashua mall. She worked in the men's suit section and arranged a deal with a number of officers in Lowell, mostly men from Davis' command staff, to get suits from her for cheap by ringing them up at extremely low prices without authorization. She was caught on video and charged with theft by deception (Skruck). Davis chose not to conduct an investigation, so it's unknown what Lowell officers were on the surveillance video.

Buckley's name was one that was frequently referenced when command staff and detectives spoke openly about the issue in roll call. Things like this were often openly talked about in Lowell, it was so commonplace that it was considered normal. None of these guys ever got in trouble and they clearly felt as though they were invincible. They never bothered to hide their illegal activities within the station, their position as members of the royalty class meant they were protected.

In spite of calls for further investigation by City Councilor Rita Mercier (Minch), the situation was buried. Coan was allowed to resign and no investigation was ever done. I think Davis couldn't allow an investigation to happen because he would have lost most of his command staff, so he made sure it didn't happen. Things like this happened all the time.

Mark Buckley took $2,000 from the department while he was assigned to the Vice/Narcotics Unit to pay for a family vacation in Florida. When Officer Pender tried to report it, he was sanctioned. Pender was later forced to write a false spending report designed to cover up money that was missing from the unit in case the unit was ever under investigation for missing funds.

These are just a few instances, the only ones that I personally know of. It may not be hard proof, but considering how Davis never hesitated to break the law to suit his needs in all other aspects of his career, it is enough to shed a reasonable doubt on his fiscal honesty as well. Davis accepted all of this money to implement community policing programs in Lowell and he received accolades for the work that he did. Community policing in Lowell looked a lot different in reality than he made it appear.

Davis did such a good job with his community policing model and falsification of police statistics that Lowell started its own police academy where local officers were sent to learn about the methods employed in Lowell. Chiefs from the surrounding communities sent their officers to Davis' academy to learn about the "hugely successful" community policing practices that Davis had implemented in Lowell.

When officers come out of the academy, the next step in the process is field training. I worked in Lowell as a field training officer, and I frequently had officers fresh out of Davis' academy assigned to me. The academy focused so much on community policing that the officers were leaving the academy without basic police skills. For example, these officers had extremely poor handcuffing skill. The utilization of good handcuffing skill is essential for officer safety. The ability to get someone under control and handcuffed swiftly saved me from having to fight with them so many times it's countless.

They also didn't really know how to write reports. These new guys said they only received a four-hour class on report writing. At the State Police academy I attended, report writing was a daily class for the entire academy. We went over report writing every day and had daily homework assignments where we wrote reports on a myriad of crimes and situations. To only receive a four-hour class on report writing was a disservice to these people and a disgrace. I spent a majority of my field training time teaching them how to write reports.

Davis' Claim to Fame

Part of the reason Ed Davis gained so much notoriety for his community policing initiatives was because of his claim that that he managed to lower crime by 50% in Lowell during his first five years in office, from 1994 to 1999. The only source of this miraculous claim is Ed Davis. There is no other source or data, just Davis' word. It is a claim that is not backed up by any facts, and I believe the statistic was actually made up. For one thing, the number kept changing. Some newspaper articles claim that Davis reduced crime by 50% while others claim it decreased by 60% (Estes). In July 2001, Congressman Meehan said crime was lowered in the city by 42% during a speech he gave honoring the department (Congressman Martin Meehan).

Crime in Lowell did decrease somewhat during those years, but based on my experience it was nowhere near as much as Davis claimed. There are a variety of reasons for this. First, the number of officers working in the city almost doubled. Naturally, crime will go down if you hire an additional 100 officers because there will be more people on the street causing the deterrence factor to go up.

It is also important to note that all of the surrounding towns reported a decrease in crime during this time period; in fact, crime started decreasing everywhere across the nation in the early to mid-nineties, and it is a trend that has continued to this day. "Both violent and property crime declined significantly between 1990 and 2008 in the 100 largest metro areas, with the largest decreases occurring in cities. Violent crime rates dropped by almost 30 percent in cities" (Kneebone). Thirty percent over 18 years is significantly less of a change than 60 percent over five years, and a much more reasonable claim.

No one has been able to decide on a logical explanation for the decrease in crime. Some claim that efforts to reduce the use of lead in the seventies caused the next generation to be less prone to violence due to decreased exposure. Others claim that Roe v. Wade led to fewer unwanted babies, thus fewer people who were inclined to fall into a life of crime. There are studies that have found increased prison populations have led to a 25% decrease in rates of crime (Palta). Another theory is that the increase in cell phone usage decreased the levels of crime. The explanations vary from reasonable to outlandish, with no definitive evidence backing any of them.

The increase in personal cell phone ownership is something I noticed having an effect on reduced appearance of crime myself while working as a police officer. Crime, especially drug crime, appeared to drop everywhere when cellular phones became readily available to the public. Suddenly the ubiquitous drug houses that littered Lowell and other cities across the country disappeared. Cell phone access eliminated the need for a fixed location or storefront for drug sales because mobile communication allowed drug dealers and buyers to meet anywhere for a benign looking and quick transaction. It enabled them always to change locations because buyers called the dealers and set up a location to meet over the phone and were readily able to contact each other on the road. This made it more difficult to track down dealers, causing drug arrests to drop. To the public, it looked like drug crime had disappeared. The drug dealing was still there, but now it was out of view.

In Lowell, this fulfilled the community policing goal of reducing the "fear of crime" and Davis was able to claim it as his success. The drugs were still there, but the citizens of Lowell couldn't see them anymore so they were no longer a problem. That was good enough for Davis, and it helped to make his ridiculous claim believable.

James Alan Fox, a crime statistics expert and professor of criminology, law, and public policy at Northeastern University, has said that, due to the fact that the crime drop has occurred everywhere, "one should be a bit skeptical of any particular police chief claiming that it is because of what his or her department is doing or any lawmaker claiming that some new legislation is responsible," (Wilson). Where was he in 2000 when Davis was making his wild claims? Unfortunately, the nationwide decrease had not become as widely recognized then, and Davis was able to get away with claiming the success as his own.

Even though crime decreased everywhere starting in 1990, Davis was the only one to claim such a large drop over such a short period of time. If Alan Fox is right and we should be skeptical of Davis claiming that it was because of his policies, then what exactly happened in Lowell during this time? Considering the fact that Davis was appointed as the police commissioner of Boston based on this claim, it is important that we examine it more closely.

There are a number of problems with Davis' wild claim that quickly become evident. One of these is that the drastic drop in crime claimed by Davis pretty much disappeared after 1999. Prior to 1999, all the records in Lowell were kept on paper and could be easily manipulated. After that, all the records became computerized and it became harder for Davis to change things in his favor. Before the switch, command staff talked openly about changing the data and "cooking the books."

If Davis decreased crime as much as he claimed, then why couldn't he maintain it after 1999? According to city-data.com, the rates of violent crimes like assaults and rapes were significantly higher in Lowell during Davis' last four years as Chief than the rest of the country. How much good did Davis really do?

Additionally there were a number of years, throughout the summer months, where it became standard practice for the shift commander to come to roll call on Saturday and Sunday and tell us not to make any arrests.

"The cell block is full and we can't bail anyone else out. Do not stop any cars, do not run any warrants, do not make any arrests. Just respond to calls, that's it."

The station in Lowell was desperately in need for an update, and we could only hold about 30 people at most in the cell block. Booking fewer people led to lowered crime statistics, and this helped bolster Davis' claim of reducing crime.

So where did this ridiculous statistic come from? What number is the right number? Why does it keep changing based on the source? My belief is that Davis made up the statistic and supported it with manipulation and lies. I feel that his supporters in the community and at the *Lowell Sun* repeated it often enough that people began to believe it. It was just all smoke and mirrors resulting from efforts to decrease the appearance of crime, and increasing the "feel good" factor of the local community. To this day, no one has exposed the statistic for the fraud that it is, and no one has investigated this claim further, in spite of Davis' inability to replicate his results in Boston (Cramer).

Due to the spectacular results that Davis claimed to achieve in Lowell, he was appointed to be a consultant on the Governor's Commission on Criminal Justice Innovation (hereafter called the

Commission). The creation of the Commission was announced in 2003 with a stated goal of coming up with "cutting-edge crime fighting techniques" for Governor Mitt Romney to implement in Massachusetts. Participants received instructions to evaluate current practices across Massachusetts to see what worked and what didn't in order to offer recommendations for improvement.

Davis received an appointment to the Urban Crime subcommittee, one of five subcommittees on the Commission. He claimed to be excited about the opportunity "to share programs that have shown results in Lowell with his counterparts on the commission, with the goal of applying them statewide" (Mehegan). Naturally, this was true, because Davis had established the first and one of the only police academies in the state that taught community policing practices (Ed Davis, Alvarez vs. Lowell, January 6, 2006, Page 38). If the programs became statewide, his academy would surely prosper.

The final report of the Commission was released in April 2004. Sure enough, the Urban Crime subcommittee recommended more emphasis on community policing and partnerships within the community, and an approach to policing that involved preventative and intervention efforts along with enforcement. It also stated that high-quality information sharing among departments was very important (Mike Laub's Website). Lots of things that Davis claimed to have implemented in Lowell, things that helped him reduce crime in Lowell, now were recommended for use statewide, influenced by his "expertise."

After the Commission published their recommendations, the Criminal Justice Policy Coalition of Massachusetts (hereafter called the Coalition) submitted a letter addressing problems with the Commission's recommendations (Healey Commission Report). There were a number of issues noted, but some are of particular interest, considering Ed Davis' history and his participation in putting these recommendations together. When Davis' police career was just starting, he worked a case where an innocent man was sent to prison for life, and it appears as though he used techniques that are very similar to the issues of concern for the coalition.

When Davis was a detective with less than five years on the job, two similar rape cases came across his desk with an ambiguous description of the perpetrator. He went to the general area of the scene of the crime presumably to find a lead (Thirty Years After Wrongful Conviction). Davis saw a man exiting a liquor store who vaguely resembled the descriptions in his files. That man was Dennis Maher, a soldier assigned to the 10th Special Forces Group at Fort Devens, in Ayer, Massachusetts. Davis stopped Maher and arrested him for possession of a small amount of marijuana. He was placed in line ups in an attempt to get the victims to identify him as the perpetrator. In one line-up, the victim did not identify Maher, so Davis had her try again, allegedly using visual clues to influence her decision. It isn't hard to believe that Davis cajoled these women to identify Maher as the suspect.

Maher had a verifiable alibi that he was at Fort Devens the night of one of the rapes. Davis displayed no knowledge of basic criminal investigation and never investigated Maher's claim. If he had, Maher would have been ruled out as suspect early on, and the police could have focused on finding the real rapist. It seems that quickly closing the case and looking good was more important than finding the truth. He was eager to get a conviction and didn't bother to stop and worry about details, such as alibis.

While conducting his investigation, Davis realized a similar unsolved crime had occurred in Ayer, and he contacted the detective in charge of that case to let her know he may have found her suspect. He shared his "bad information" that Maher had been identified by the victims in a line-up, gleaned from his unsavory methods of fact-finding. That officer, Nancy Harris, had also been involved with several wrongful convictions, even one that made it to the big screen as a movie (McCabe). Her ethics are clearly on the same level as those of Ed Davis, and I believe the two worked together to convict Maher with no qualms about the knowledge that the other was manipulating evidence, because that was just how they did things.

Maher was sentenced to life in prison and ended up spending 19 years in jail on these charges before DNA testing exonerated him. When Maher was freed from prison, Davis refused to apologize, claiming no wrongdoing (Cramer). The prosecutor on the case, J.W. Carney, met with Maher at the first possible opportunity to express his regret (Thirty Years After Wrongful Conviction: Reflections from Exoneree Dennis Maher). Even if you believed you did nothing wrong, wouldn't you at least feel guilt for sending an innocent man to jail for 19 years? Wouldn't you want at least to apologize for being a part of it? A decent man would.

Maher filed a lawsuit against the cities of Lowell and Ayer. In his case against Lowell, he accused Ed Davis and Officer Garrett Sheehan of "a series of abuses, including falsifying a police report and trying to undermine Maher's alibi" (Cramer). Aliza Kaplan, the attorney from the Innocence Project who represented Maher, was quoted as saying "knowing this case as in-depth as I do, it's quite possible there was some major wrongdoing" (Lafleur).

The lawsuit was filed after Maher had been completely exonerated by DNA evidence, after DNA evidence had shown that at least two of the three crimes Maher had been convicted of were actually perpetrated by different suspects. In spite of this, an article in the *Lowell Sun* reports that Maher sued the city of Lowell for crimes "he *says* he didn't commit" (Lafleur). Once a person is exonerated by DNA, it means they did not commit the crime, however this small play on words by the staff at the *Sun*, who were in Davis' pocket, served to make Davis look better.

The case against Lowell was ultimately settled out of court, but that doesn't mean Davis is innocent. All of the things Maher accused Davis of doing in his lawsuit are very similar to actions he has been accused of by numerous others throughout his career, making it is easier and easier to believe Davis purposefully manipulated the case in order to solve it quickly and look good to his superiors. It's one thing to be accused of doing something by one person and claim that he has lied. However, that stance becomes more and more difficult to prove as the number of people accusing you of the same thing, independently of each other, grows.

When I took Davis and the City of Lowell to court, Davis expressed his faith in DNA testing and his detective ethics perfectly.

> "(O)ne thing I've known in police work is the stuff that you see on television, the C.S.I., D.N.A. stuff doesn't really solve crime. The way we solve crime in police agencies, is *people tell us who did it*. The other stuff is all an adjunct to that" (Alvarez vs. Lowell, January 25, 2006, P. 150).

That's exactly how Davis gets to the bottom of things, he listens to what people tell him. My experience is that those who are in his favor can say whatever they want and he takes that as the truth. I don't think evidence means anything to this man. After all the people who have been freed from prison for wrongful charges since DNA testing became more accessible, one would think he would take it a little more seriously, treat it with a little more respect.

One of the issues noted by the Coalition was that sharing information across departments could be problematic because police reports are often subject to bias and opinion and could be filled with misinformation. The Coalition was concerned that there was nothing in place to ensure the quality of the information shared, and nothing to prevent abuse or misuse of the information contained in the files. It addressed the issue of wrongful convictions, and how police misinformation had contributed to this horrific and growing problem across the country.

Police agencies should and have shared information over the years, but like anything it has to be utilized properly and professionally. There are definitely instances in recent history where cross-agency information sharing could have prevented a disaster. The problem that concerned the Coalition was the potential for the information to be bad or to be abused. An example is when a detective manipulates a police investigation to get a victim to identify the perpetrator, and then shares that false information with another department to get the person charged with additional crimes that he/she didn't commit.

The Coalition also expressed concern over the Commission's recommendation for increased reliance on forensic technology because there are reports of labs falsifying their analyses of evidence intentionally, and those reports could prove problematic if they were shared with a larger group of law enforcement professionals. A dirty detective intent on getting a quick conviction would have no problem manipulating the evidence in this manner.

The entire case of Dennis Maher shows how the problems with the recommendations made by the Commission are very real concerns. Davis participated in cross-agency information sharing when he was investigating the rape cases for which Dennis Maher was falsely accused. Davis and the detective in Ayer manipulated evidence in order wrongfully to convict a man of rape, and then shared that information in order to ensure he was sent to prison. It is my opinion that, if the incident had occurred in 2003 instead of 1983, that Davis would have used his influence to falsify the DNA reports in order to ensure Maher was convicted. It has happened before in other parts of the country (Vibes).

A short time after Maher was released in 2003, Davis ordered the Criminal Bureau to start disposing of old cases. Captain Bobbie Demoura, who was in charge of the bureau, rented an industrial shredder to get rid of all the old police reports. A detective in the bureau spoke with me and noted that they started shredding reports from the 1980s, coincidentally from around the same time frame as Maher's case, when Davis worked as a detective. Clearly the Innocence Project that helped free Maher wasn't going to be working on any more cases out of Lowell. How many of these were cases Davis worked on where he used similar tactics to ensure his suspect ended up behind bars?

The Trial

We knew the case was going to be in court for a long time by the time we finally got there. The trial date was set for January 9, 2006. We expected it would be at least two weeks, and it ended up lasting for three. This is a lot longer than the average trial and required a lot more from the jurors than an average trial would. It can be very difficult to find a truly high quality jury when you're limited by the fact that the jurors have to be able to walk away from their lives for three whole weeks. The courts provide a small stipend for longer cases, but it is a very small stipend. In the movies and on television, the viewer is given the impression that lawyers pick a jury based on interviews with potential jurors to determine who is likely to side with their case. But the reality, at least for my case, was different. My jury was chosen primarily by their ability to sit through several weeks of court hearings without it negatively impacting their lives, although there was also effort by the judge to weed out anyone who would be obviously prejudiced toward either side.

The jury was made up of twelve women and two men, and most of them were either retired or college students. All were white except for one elderly black woman. After the trial, I had an opportunity to speak with the jurors and they stated that this woman rarely spoke and basically had no input in any of the jury decisions. This was not exactly the ideal jury for a discrimination case. This worried me some, but I felt my case was so strong and I clearly had all the elements to prove discrimination, so I hoped it wouldn't affect the final outcome. I had to make do with what I had and hope for the best.

The city's lawyer, Brian Leahy, painted a picture of me as a disgruntled and insubordinate cop who was playing the race card because I didn't want to do my job. He basically said there was no such thing as discrimination, which is a commonly held belief by a good portion of the population in this country. Although Judge Fishman conducted himself professionally, I got the sense early on that he, too, adhered to this common misnomer. I could almost see him thinking to himself, "Oh, right, another 'discrimination' case." You could tell by the questions he asked that he didn't believe me at all. As the case continued, however, his interest and belief in my claim increased, and the tone and type of questions changed.

One of the first issues addressed was the establishment of whether or not I was a Hispanic minority. The city attorneys had already won the first MCAD case by presenting that I was white based on my birth certificate, so this was their strategy once again. Because I have never met my biological father, it was established that I could not testify to my own ethnic background because I had no firsthand knowledge of who I was.

I would like to present the story of my ethnic background to clear things up. My biological father is Agrippino Alvarez. In 1957, he was finishing up his degree at Harvard Law School when he met my mother, Ellen Godimis, a white, third-generation, Greek-American. She was taking art classes at Harvard. The two met and married, and shortly thereafter my mother became pregnant with me. Alvarez was a Filipino national, and he told Ellen he was part Spanish and had lived in Spain as a youth. I would learn later that he was a skilled womanizer and had fathered children all over the world.

Soon after he graduated from Harvard, he left Ellen. She was left behind in 1958 as a single mother with a half-breed child. She had already been disowned by her family for marrying outside her race, and she didn't have a lot of support. On top of everything, Ellen was a damaged soul from events that occurred long before I was born. Her mental stability was always in question. By the time I was ten months old, she was under tremendous stress and became suicidal. I was taken in by my foster parents, with whom I would live until I joined the Marines at seventeen. Mildred and Stephen Phyllis became my mom and dad for the remainder of my life. My mom, Millie, was British-Canadian and Native American, thus her skin tone was similar to my own. My dad, Steve, grew up in an orphanage in the 1920s, and he had no knowledge of his background, but he was clearly white. Although I knew Ellen and would visit her when I was young, we really were estranged.

Throughout my life, people, primarily white people, have questioned what my race was. I identified myself as Spanish and Greek for years until the middle of the 80s, when the word Hispanic arose as an identifier for race. After that, I identified myself as Hispanic because that was the term that most closely fit with my background. After all, "Hispanic" denotes people of mixed races and I'm a Hispanic who actually has Spanish DNA.

When the MCAD pronounced I was not Hispanic because my birth certificate stated that I was white, I started a genealogy search to demonstrate my heritage in court. I knew Alvarez graduated from Harvard Law, so I began by contacting the alumni offices there. Harvard's records showed that he had a law practice in a suburb outside of Chicago. I called the town hall hoping to locate a death certificate that may have his ethnicity listed, but I didn't have any luck there.

Ellen told me that she heard he had died early in the 1990s, and that he may have other children. My wife suggested that I try calling information for Alvarez in that town to see if a child of his lived nearby. Information had only one Alvarez listed in the area and I called it. My wife's suggestion paid off, and the listed Alvarez was actually one of my half-siblings.

I found that I had ten half-siblings living across the country. They told me that when Alvarez died, they discovered files in his office desk on all the children that he fathered. There was a file about me in the desk, and most of the family already knew I existed.

The oldest of Alvarez's children was a daughter who he fathered in Spain as a teenager. Today she would be in her eighties, and is presumed to still live in Spain. He then went on to father eight children with his wife Rose. These children range in age from their mid-sixties to their early forties. I fall in the middle of this range, which means Alvarez was married to Rose long before he went to Harvard and married Ellen. After he left Ellen, he returned to Rose and had four more children with her. The last of Alvarez's children is a daughter who was born out of wedlock and lives in Florida. I have met the Chicago and Florida crew and they are a loving, wonderful family. They are very accepting of me.

When I questioned them about the family background, they explained that Alvarez's mother, my grandmother, had very dark skin with straight black hair. They were not sure of her nationality, however. In 2015, I had my DNA examined and it came back that I am forty percent Southern European, a mix of Spanish and Greek. Fifteen percent of my DNA comes from the Middle East, Syria and Turkey area. Twenty-five percent comes from Southern Africa, Mozambique and Madagascar. The final twenty percent comes from

Central and Northern Asia, a mix of Chinese and Russian from the Siberian region.

The city's lawyers worked very hard to prove their claim that I was white and that everyone I worked with saw me that way. They even went so far as to have a woman from the Department of Civil Service testify that three weeks after I became a police officer, I drove to Boston and had my ethnicity changed from Hispanic to White. When questioned further, she testified that there were no witnesses to verify that I was ever there at the Boston office, and there were no documents with my signature. She testified that a computer readout indicated codes that the change was made by me in person at my request. This was clearly not possible because I was in the state police academy at that time, a six-week program of which I never missed a single day. I got on the witness stand and explained you can't take a vacation day or call in sick during the academy.

She was questioned as to how civil service identifies an individual's race and her response was that each person is allowed to identify his/her race himself/herself. I identified myself as Hispanic in 1986 when I took the civil service exam, twenty years before the trial. I don't know how much clearer that could be. I get to identify myself; not Davis, not other police chiefs, not the city attorney, but me. It's a pretty simple concept. After this I thought the issue had been settled, if I self-identified as Hispanic, and that's how the civil service identified a person's ethnicity, then it was clear that I was Hispanic as far as the police were concerned. Right?

Her testimony also raised some flags. Did anyone know that you can change your race? Who actually does that? My lawyer asked if she knew of any time that anyone else changed his/her race because it appeared like a rather unusual thing to do. She said no, that I was the only one she knew of who had done so. The only person who ever changed his race was the same person who had filed for a racial discrimination civil lawsuit against the city of Lowell and the soon-to-be Police Commissioner of Boston. Based on this testimony, it was abundantly clear that someone had underhandedly manipulated my records in order to give their case some clout. Unfortunately for them, this backfired and showed them to be nothing more than the liars that they really are. Based on my police experience there is only one clear suspect who would benefit from this change and possessed the level of authority and influence to coerce the altering of my records. This person also has a history of being accused of manipulating evidence. Who would you suspect?

The Lowell Police Department definitely viewed me as a minority officer, even though several officers took the stand and said they viewed me as white. When I transferred from Waltham Police Department to the Lowell Police Department, I frequently got called on by the police dispatchers to translate for Spanish-speaking calls. The department assumed I spoke Spanish based on my physical appearance and my last name. Because I was raised by white parents, I never learned Spanish, but it took a little while for the Lowell Police dispatchers to figure that out.

Also, over the course of my career, there were at least ten occasions where I responded to a call and upon arrival the caller refused to talk to me.

"I'm not going to talk to you. I want a white cop." "I don't need you. I need a real cop."

I would radio back that I had cleared the call and stated that the caller was requesting a white officer. But no one in the department saw me as a minority.

The city tried to establish that I couldn't be Hispanic because I didn't speak Spanish and that this demonstrated that discrimination could not have occurred. Not everyone who identifies as Hispanic speaks Spanish, even if he/she has Spanish heritage and was raised by parents whose native language is Spanish. Heritage is not the language you speak; many people of varying backgrounds do not speak the language of their homeland.

The defense lawyers didn't stop there, however. I mentioned that they manipulated my civil service record. They also convinced a number of officers to say on the stand that they viewed me as white in spite of the numerous examples that I had showing that others saw me as a minority. They even went so far as to use the names I gave my daughters against me, claiming that I couldn't be Hispanic because my daughter's names were not Spanish enough. It was pretty unbelievable the types of arguments they came up with to prove that I was not Hispanic.

Additionally, I was invited to go to the minority officer's meeting held by Davis when it clearly said on the invitation that the meeting was for minority officers only. While in court, Davis tried to claim that I had been invited by mistake because the meeting had been thrown together hastily and his secretary must have invited me by accident (Robert Alvarez v. City of Lowell, Jan. 25, 2006, P. 3). His excuse didn't hold up because I was never approached and asked to leave, and I was invited to the second meeting.

Unfortunately, at least three jurors bought it to an extent, and it was not determined that the actions taken against me were due to racial discrimination. In order to win the charges in my case, I needed twelve out of the fourteen to agree with my position. With a jury of thirteen white jurors and one elderly black female juror, my lawyer and I repeatedly noticed that they did not appear to be understanding the issues as a group.

The city lawyers' defense focused so much on proving that I wasn't a minority, they appeared to forget that I was also suing for retaliation. The city continued to punish me after my case was filed. Throughout the case, every time the city's lawyers believed that they had established that I was white, they called for a bench meeting and tried to convince the judge that the case should be thrown out. They did this again and again.

I could almost write an entire chapter on Ed Davis' testimony because it was filled with so many lies and contradictions. The whole time he was on the stand, he very conveniently forgot any of the details of my case that could cause any problems for him. This could be believable, except he had a remarkable memory for very minute details of events that happened that painted him in a more favorable light. He couldn't remember when he filed for my suspension, or whether or not he actually saw me with the other SWAT members at the hangar during the Marchionda incident. He couldn't remember anything about my case if it was something he had previously lied about when my lawyer presented evidence to the contrary.

Davis also constantly contradicted himself. At one point during the trial, he claimed that the massive amount of lies in his deposition were due to him being "mistaken" because he had not reviewed my file prior to getting deposed. He stated earlier that he reviewed the internal affairs report from my file. When he was confronted about the fact that the report didn't exist, he claimed that another report that was in my file that he never reviewed looked like an internal affairs report, which is why he testified to its existence in his deposition.

This brings up the question, what type of Police Chief wouldn't review the file of the officer he was about to be deposed on before going in? Wouldn't it make sense to be sure of all of the details before testifying to them in a court of law? It does make sense, and it is probably what actually happened because later in the trial Davis claimed that he did look at my file before the deposition.

At one point, he said he did not know when he actually spoke with me about the State Trooper incident. During his deposition and at other points during the trial, he said that he spoke to me the night that it happened. His claim was that I asked the trooper to drive me back to the station because I was refusing to work with him. Davis claimed he spoke with me that night to tell me that I had to follow orders, and that I returned to duty with the trooper after his talk with me. As more evidence came out, however, he suddenly didn't remember if he spoke with me that night, or sometime after that. He couldn't recall any of the conversations for sure, but recalled I swore at him and I appeared mentally unstable. He denied swearing at me when questioned about it.

Davis testified to being confused that day when I was in his office, because he didn't understand how an officer who had only been on the force two or three years could harbor such strong feelings toward the state police. He later testified that he remembered hearing about the jewelry store shooting, an incident, which had occurred over ten years before he had me in his office that day. If he knew this, there is no telling where his statement that I was a "rookie" with only two or three years on the force came from. He also testified a number of other times to knowledge of my experience.

Davis said that he was the person who hired me and assigned me to SWAT in the first place. I was hired and appointed to SWAT two weeks before Davis became Chief, by the previous Chief. When confronted with the paperwork showing that this was a lie, he claimed to be mistaken again. His reasoning was that he was so involved in the hiring process that he forgot that it was actually the previous chief who did so. He had looked over my file with his predecessor before I was hired in order to provide input, and that was why he thought he had actually hired me. It's rather interesting to note that a short time later he testified to knowledge that his predecessor had spoken with the chief of Waltham before deciding to hire me, and that the conversation between the two chiefs had occurred without Davis and before he had been given access to my file. This means I was actually hired before Davis saw my file; his input was, at best, an afterthought.

Davis also said a number of things that did not make sense. For example, he said that my actions during Marchionda's funeral left him deeply concerned about my mental state. He never ordered me to have any type of psychiatric or psychological examination as a result of his concern. He was so concerned that he never spoke to me about it or directed a supervisor to speak to me. I was allowed to continue on SWAT for another six months and I was kept on patrol for years after the incident. Why would he allow an unstable officer to handle a gun and arrest suspects who were sometimes armed and dangerous? Maybe he was not actually concerned about my mental state, he just needed an excuse for his actions.

At one point during his testimony, Davis actually said, "if someone (a police officer) starts what could be a physical confrontation, it's incumbent that the other officer walk away" (Alvarez vs Lowell, P.61, January 26, 2001). Marisa and I looked at each other with disbelief, and then I looked over at Judge Fishman. He could not hide his look of shock when Davis said this; it was priceless. The judge then looked directly at me and gave me a huge grin. Davis completely forgot the fact that I walked away that night when Kennedy tried to start a fight. Davis' statement was in reference to a different altercation that had occurred between two white officers in the department, but he might as well have been talking about my case. I walked away that day and Kennedy pursued me.

My lawyer questioned Davis about the other men in the department who wanted to get on SWAT. She got him to say that they were all rookies, but he defended it because "the rookies who are fresh out of the academy have had military experience, have been in a theater of (war), have had much more experience than someone like Robert Alvarez in highly critical (incidents) involving firearms" (Court Transcripts P. 85 January 26, 2001).

Davis conveniently forgot that I had six years in the Marine Corps Reserves as a platoon sergeant and was airborne and scuba qualified. I had also received a meritorious mast award for leadership while attached to 1st Battalion Recon. I was originally recruited to the SWAT Team specifically because of my military background. I also had several years of experience on the SWAT team, I had been on more than 120 operations, and I had been a team leader or in the number one position, which is first man through the door, on most of those operations. I also had nine years of experience as a firearms instructor and had been a SWAT instructor in charge of running training a number of times. This was all information in my file, which he said he reviewed. Additionally, it had all been introduced to the court before Davis took the stand.

A rookie, even one who had military experience, was still unlikely to have more experience than me in "highly critical incidents involving firearms," The fact is no one from Lowell who Davis assigned to the SWAT Team after I was removed has any military combat experience, none. Once again, his claims just did not hold up.

Unfortunately, Davis' testimony was so full of holes, that it can be tiresome to speak about it, read about it, or hear about it. However, it is important that people understand how far this man was willing to go to protect himself, and how convinced he was of his own invincibility. I believe he felt he was above the law and he knew it. He seemed to think he could say anything, lie about anything, and his words would never be questioned. Based on my experience, no one would never investigate him for perjury, no matter what he did or said.

He tried to paint himself as a hero by claiming he worked with the minority officers in the department by creating a liaison, because minority officers "wanted someone that they felt comfortable with speaking to about issues" (Court Transcripts P. 26 January 26, 2001). He appointed Hickman after the officers protested that they wished to pick someone themselves via a vote, and that they did not trust Hickman. Otero, Pender and I all testified that we had absolutely no trust in Larry Hickman.

When discussing the Marchionda incident, he said he spoke to Roarke and Stanley about my behavior during his deposition, but in court he said he spoke with Sergeant Taylor. During the trial he said he was told by Sergeant Taylor that I was directly involved, but later said he wasn't sure if I was involved.

He made statements that immediately contradicted previous statements. For example, when asked about my outside employment, he said he didn't remember who told him that I was doing executive protection in Lowell. My lawyer responded:

> "So you have just a vague recollection of somebody saying he might work in Lowell someday?"
>
> No I was told specifically that this company did contracts where he was doing executive protection in the City of Lowell.

> Well you remember specifically being told. You can't tell me who it was?
> No I can't." (Alvarez vs Lowell, P. 101, Jan 26).

I don't think I fully understood the influence Davis had until the time during and after my trial. He managed to get people who I thought were on my side to testify against me, and later his influence got people who I thought were my friends to turn against me. Multiple high-ranking officials from the Lowell Police Department got on the stand and committed perjury. My lawyer provided evidence to prove they were lying, and they either folded under pressure or pretended not to know what she was talking about. I eventually came to realize that everyone was afraid of Davis because they knew he would retaliate against anyone who crossed him. These officers may have been on my side, but they didn't dare show it for fear of having their own careers destroyed as a result.

Demoura took the stand and testified that his investigation into the Kennedy incident was complete and proper. He said he determined that I struck Kennedy even though nothing in his reports stated that this was what happened. He held this position even when he was faced with the fact that most of the reports were turned in after he concluded that a lengthy suspension was required.

"I stand by the results of my investigation," he said resolutely.

When confronted by my lawyer with facts that confronted his lies, he shrugged.

"I don't know."

Demoura also testified that I was difficult to supervise, but when pressed he had nothing to back up this statement. When asked if he ever addressed me directly about being difficult, he said no.

Over the years, I really had no contact with Demoura except for one incident. Command staff personnel were famous for driving around the city and pointing out criminal activity that patrolmen were missing. It was something they did to demonstrate their powers of observation in order to bolster their belief that they were superior crime fighters, deserving of their privileged positions. One evening the radio cracked with Demoura's best commanding voice.

"I want that drug dealer on the corner of Merrimack and Aiken arrested."

"Lowell to Captain Demoura. What do you need?"

"Get that drug dealer off the corner."

Dispatch responded, "Copy Captain. Lowell to Car 10 can you respond?"

Unfortunately, I was in Car 10. Merrimack and Aiken wasn't in my sector, but I had to respond to the call.

"10 copied, can I get a description?"

"The drug dealer, get him off the corner!" Demoura barked, refusing to give anything more.

When I arrived I found a Hispanic man with a small backpack standing alone on the corner.

I approached him. "Hey man, what's up?" I asked.

"Not much," he responded inquisitively, obviously wondering why I had approached him.

"Hey, sorry to bother you," I replied, "but someone seems to be wondering why you're here on the corner."

"I'm just waiting for the bus. I live right there." He pointed to the fourth house down on Aiken Street.

"Where ya headed tonight?"

"I clean the law offices downtown at night."

"This is the last bus for tonight. How do you get home?"

"I walk," he responded matter-of-factly.

"Can I just see some ID please?" I asked. "Then I'll leave you be."

He produced a license and I ran his information. Dispatch advised me that his license was active with an address on Aiken Street. He had no BOP (board of probation), which indicated no criminal record.

Knowing Demoura and the rest of the shift was listening, I radioed in.

"Car 10 is clear, no report."

Demoura chimed in. "Get him off the corner!" he demanded.

"He's just waiting for the bus," I replied calmly. "He'll be off the corner when it arrives."

I knew this would piss him off, but I wasn't going to harass this guy just because he wanted me to. The radio went silent.

If I was obedient and hoped to maybe receive a "gift" in the future, I think I would have had to placate Demoura by thoroughly harassing, patting down, and humiliating this man who was simply waiting for the bus. This was an example of how I was "difficult to supervise" as he testified to. This is the only example of racial profiling I had ever seen. Although the department reeked of internal discrimination, I never found that officers targeted people just based on race alone. Racism is cloaked in a completely different facade. To my knowledge, racial profiling as depicted in the media doesn't really exist as it is portrayed.

Buckley's testimony was more of the same. He testified that he was there and saw me strike Kennedy. Because Tom Rielly's office refused to press charges against Davis for perjury, Buckley knew he was free from any repercussions and added a new twist to his story. He testified that I got right up into Kennedy's face while screaming at him, which constituted an assault, and that Kennedy had no alternative but to strike me. This was never mentioned before, Buckley just got creative in court that day and said whatever he thought would get a response from the jury and make his story more believable. Buckley was also questioned about the felony car stop procedure and to describe in detail his own experience with felony car stops. He testified he had never actually done one. This was completely different from his testimony during the city manager's hearing where he testified he had done "hundreds" of felony car stops.

During my testimony, we didn't address Buckley's lying at length, because we planned to have Laferriere get on the stand after Buckley to refute what he had said. Just as Laferriere was about to take the stand, the city attorney requested a sidebar discussion with the judge. It was a lengthy discussion and at the end, Judge Fishman blocked Laferriere from testifying. This was a huge blow to our case and quite a disappointment.

Chief Rick Stanley of the North Andover Police Department was the control chief for the NEMLEC SWAT team and was called upon to testify about my conduct during the funerals. Stanley was one of my witnesses, but he and Davis have been close personal friends for many years, and the city hoped to use him against me. It didn't work out quite as they had planned, however. Stanley was forced to testify I had nothing to do with any disruption at the airport hangar or the funeral home.

When questioned about my minority status, Stanley testified that there has never been a minority on the SWAT team. He stated he always considered me to be white and he considered the name Alvarez to be a white name. This was a complete lie. In the early 90s during SWAT training Stanley paid us a visit with Jim Rice of the Boston Red Sox. Rice lived in North Andover and Stanley wanted to show off the team to him. He introduced us all to Rice one by one. Upon coming to me, he said,

"This is Bob Alvarez, one of our Hispanic officers."

Jim Rice is a black celebrity and it was the first time that Stanley had noted my ethnicity. He clearly saw me as a minority.

Stanley was questioned about my performance on SWAT.

"He was ok," he responded.

"Just ok? Wasn't he a team leader?" Marisa pushed him to be clearer.

"Oh everyone is a team leader," he said. "Anyone at any scene can be a team leader in the absence of someone of rank, and there really isn't any really responsibility associated with the title."

"Why was he always put in the number one position on operations then?" Marisa asked.

"I don't know," he shrugged.

He was forced to admit I had a lot of military experience that helped with training and that I was in excellent physical shape and was an excellent shot.

When questioned about Crowley's poor performance, Stanley denied it.

"Crowley was excellent," he said.

Lieutenant Roarke was now deputy chief at the Chelmsford Police Department, and, like Stanley, was friends with Davis. He was friends with me as well, but on a different level. Roarke and Davis were equals in the police hierarchy, and they would both always be my superior. We went to each other's houses and visited socially, but he would always be above me. I had been counting on Roarke to testify in my favor, but he didn't end up being as strong of a witness as I had anticipated.

When Roarke took the stand, he testified that I had no part in any desecration of Marchionda's body and that I had not been involved in any inappropriate conduct. He stated that I had been a team leader and led training for the SWAT team. He confirmed that I received two distinguished service awards and a citation for gallantry from NEMLEC. He testified that I had been in deadly force encounters, "several times," and that I had utilized a lower level of force to take suspects into custody rather than going directly to deadly force. In other words, I avoided killing a suspect in high stress situations where the use of deadly force would have been considered acceptable based on the actions of the suspect.

He testified that he did approach Davis and requested I return to the team. When questioned about my performance, he stated that I was good. That was all, he wouldn't go into any specifics. When he was asked about my status as the only minority on the team, Roarke stated, "I don't know about that. I don't look at people that way."

I spoke with Roarke briefly at the end of the day, as I was confused about his testimony.

"I'm sorry," he shrugged. "That's the best I could do. I need to be careful, sorry."

A few months earlier a SWAT team member had told me that he had second-hand information that Davis had threatened Roarke somehow. I had spoken with Roarke about testifying in my trial and I asked him if he, in fact, had been threatened by Davis. Roarke denied it at the time, but his testimony and apology afterwards led me to believe otherwise.

Chief Bob Silva of the Reading Police Department, who had been the commander of NEMLEC RRT and SWAT while I was on the team, took the stand and his testimony appeared as though he had been coached or advised to say something bad about me.

The city attorney asked Silva a number of questions about me that led the jury to believe that I did not follow orders and needed to be secretly watched due to his concern about my behavior. He wouldn't actually come out and specifically say he thought I had a bad attitude or didn't follow orders though, he just went along with the line of questioning.

When Marisa cross-examined him, she pushed for clarification. "And what about Alvarez's attitude?"

"He was well trained, in good shape, and an aggressive and independent thinker," he said before pausing to think. "In other words, he would question a lot of the procedures that we followed, making suggestions, recommendations" (Alvarez vs.Lowell, P. 71, January 27).

He said this behavior concerned him, and that he was worried that I might not follow orders. Might not. When asked if I had ever disobeyed a direct order, he stated that he never said that. He then admitted that all of my questioning, suggestions, and recommendations that concerned him had only occurred during training and that I never once refused to follow an order. If he had been coached to speak about me negatively, his lies couldn't stand up to questioning because they were so thin.

Before becoming a police officer, Silva was a barber who cut hair for a living. He had no military or tactical experience. During some SWAT operations, he leaned heavily on my suggestions and was comfortable letting me take the lead because I was confident and capable where he wasn't. His testimony was a complete disgrace.

Angel Otero took the stand and testified to the fact that he was charged with sexual harassment when there was no victim. He also asserted that this was what caused him to be passed over for promotion. Dave Pender also took the stand and testified about the "bus incident," and how Davis used lies and manipulation in the investigation.

Pender testified to finding Jeff Geoffroy's police department pay stub at a drug dealer's house during a drug raid and to the fact that the drug dealer had a police scanner with the Vice Unit's secret radio frequency on it. When Davis was questioned as to why there was no Internal Affairs investigation or discipline or firing, his response was drug addiction was a disease and he couldn't discipline Geoffroy for a medical issue.

After Pender's testimony, I happened to call the station. I got Jack Cullen on the phone at the main desk.

"You should know that Geoffroy heard about Pender's testimony and he is furious, looking to fight you," he said. "You should talk to Kenny Shaw, he saw Geoffroy going nuts in the locker room looking for you."

I called Shaw, and he confirmed what Cullen had told me. I thought it was interesting that Geoffroy was going after me and not Pender. Geoffroy knew Kennedy got away with hitting me and Geoffroy was in the same royalty class as Kennedy. He probably felt safer going after me than Pender. I told Marisa the situation, and she in turn reported it to Captain Taylor, who said he would conduct an investigation.

Tommy Kennedy was now a captain in the Lowell Police Department. When he got on the stand, you could physically see he was nervous. Marisa went after him right away, asking him question after question about the felony car stop the night he assaulted me.

"But he yelled at me! He yelled at me!" Kennedy repeatedly responded. You could see he was starting to panic, darting his eyes around the room looking for some kind of escape. Just as he started to cry, Leahy sprung to his feet.

"Uh...Uh...Objection!"

"What grounds?" a puzzled Judge Fishman blurted out.

"Uh...uh...badgering the witness!"

Judge Fishman had been watching Kennedy spellbound, as we all were. It was such a pitiful spectacle, no one could really believe what they were seeing. Then the judge looked at Leahy incredulously.

"Overruled!"

"Well, you're under oath here," Marisa said, gently.

"I understand..." he whimpered.

"You have to respond," the court reporter had to state as his testimony continued.

Later, even the judge had to egg him on.

"You have to say yes or no," he said as Kennedy continued to be questioned. (Com of Ma Superior Court C.A. no MICV2002-04841 vol VI p188)

I couldn't believe he was crying again. This kid was getting promoted at an astronomical rate and he couldn't even testify without crying, while I was still fighting to get back positions I had lost when he attacked me. I was supposed to be the mentally unstable one not fit for a leadership position. But here was Kennedy, the one they promoted, blubbering on the stand like a baby. This was pathetic. He was a grown man and he was a police captain.

Previously, at the civil service trial, Kennedy testified that he had done ten felony car stops. After some lengthy questioning by Marisa, it was revealed that this was Kennedy's first felony car stop.

"How close was Alvarez when he spoke to you that night?" she continued.

"He was more than an arm's length away," Kennedy replied, clearly unaware of Buckley's testimony that I was in his face, forcing him to hit me.

I hadn't told the jury that Kennedy cried when he attacked me. I didn't think they would believe me. I did say that I held his arms down like a child having a tantrum, but that was as far as I went in explaining how childlike his behavior was. Then he cried on the stand in front of everyone during a very basic examination. His extreme sensitivity was clear to everyone in attendance.

When Lowell started its own police academy, I put in for one of the academy instructor positions. Lavallee requested that I submit my instructor and teaching background as part of the application. While I was a platoon sergeant in the Marines, I instructed and trained my platoon in squad tactics, weapons training, call for fire, land navigation, rappelling, Arctic combat skiing, combat surveillance radar, and seismic intrusion. As a police officer, I had actively been a firearms instructor for nine years, and I was also a defensive tactics instructor and training instructor for the RRT. I was also instrumental in starting the police motorcycle program in Lowell and worked as a motorcycle instructor for many classes. Finally, I taught firearms, SWAT tactics, ballistic shield tactics, and rappelling on the SWAT team. I had extensive experience working as an instructor that spanned more than a decade.

The two academy positions went to Crowley and Hickman. Hickman had no instructor certifications, but he was black and a Davis crony, so it looked good politically. As an academy instructor, Hickman taught the felony car stop. I was told that he often referred to the Kennedy incident, telling students that what I did was wrong and an example of what not to do. Apparently he directly used my name in classes and said that I started the fight and was mentally unstable. It sounds like he echoed the story Davis had been telling, as an obedient crony would do. When rookie officers were assigned to me for field training, they were all apprehensive because of the rumors spread by academy instructors. After working with me a short time, they quickly came to realize it was bullshit and they shared what they had been told with me.

When my attorney asked Crowley about his instructor background, he spoke of his extensive experience coaching junior varsity boys wrestling and Pop Warner football.

Marisa stopped him. "No, no Sergeant Crowley. What is your police instructor experience?"

"Well I assisted with a defensive tactics class once."

"So that's it. That's all?"

"Yes."

Crowley was a sergeant at the time of the trial and he lied on the stand as well. He stated he hadn't been involved in the Marchionda incident at all. His claim was that each family had been assigned a liaison from Lowell and he had escorted Sullivan's body to Westford. He did say he stopped in at Dracut, where Marchionda was, briefly. However, he claimed that he left immediately because he had things to attend to. This was a complete lie. Crowley was with the SWAT Team the entire time in SWAT uniform. He did not escort Sullivan's casket to Westford and he was with the team in Dracut for all of the events of that day.

Previously I testified that I presented Davis with the proposal for the new guns, and that Davis handed my proposal over to Crowley. Davis testified that he didn't remember getting this proposal from me, but he did state that Timmy Crowley handled the proposal and took the lead in changing over to the new guns. When questioned, Crowley said he had nothing to do with the new gun program. This too was clearly a lie. A copy of my original gun proposal had already been introduced into evidence. I suspect he lied about not being involved because he knew he wouldn't have been able to go into details of the gun proposal because it wasn't his. If he was questioned further about it, he wouldn't have had the answers.

During questioning, he couldn't remember that I had ever been a team leader on SWAT stating "I don't know". However, he was able to remember that he had been a team leader.

"As a sergeant, what is your opinion of Alvarez's performance?" Leahy, the city lawyer asked.

"Bobby thinks a lot of himself," he said. He didn't clarify.

At another point he stated, "He has nominated himself for awards." This was an interesting twist to the letter of inquiry I sent to the Awards Committee, which, by the way, was something he had no first-hand knowledge of. As a sergeant, there was no reason for him to know about it at all.

Marisa and I planned to follow up Crowley's testimony with Sergeant George Thistle from the Wakefield Police Department to counter any lies or negative testimony. Thistle was going to support the fact that Crowley rarely showed up to training and was a complete failure at SWAT Roundup in Florida. He was also going to testify how I saved his life during the Westford jewelry store shooting. But Crowley's performance on the stand was so poor it stood on its own merit. We were now coming to the end of the third week of the trial, and we believed we didn't want to add any more witnesses or add to the trial length, so we decided not to use him.

The only person who actually told the truth and stood up for me in court was Jack Davis, Ed Davis' brother. He was there the night of the Kennedy incident and he testified that I had done nothing wrong. He testified he was present when I approached Kennedy and asked if he had ever done a felony car stop. He said I did nothing inappropriate as far as he could see and backed up my story. He also said that Buckley was not there when everything happened. Jack testified that he had been promoted to sergeant a few years later and that he had been my supervisor for many years. He verified that I worked one of the busiest sections of the city and that I averaged a hundred to a hundred and thirty arrests a year, mostly felony arrests.

"Was Alvarez ever disrespectful, or did he ever refuse an order?" my lawyer asked.

"Absolutely not, he is a very solid cop."

It seems as though Jack Davis couldn't be manipulated by his brother, like everyone else. It appeared Jack and I were the only ones who weren't afraid of Ed Davis.

The Verdict

On the final day of trial before jury deliberation, Judge Fishman needed to present the jury with all of the final instructions. Throughout the trial, the judge would always call for breaks because it was hard for everyone to stay focused. But on the last day, he read through all of the lengthy instructions with no break. I looked over at the jurors at one point and saw they were all fading. I was getting lost in what the judge was saying myself. The jury was tired and you could sense their attention was waning when the applicable rules and laws were being presented. When Judge Fishman ended that day, we were all exhausted. Even the stenographer was spent.

"I can't believe he didn't take a break," she said. "I couldn't have kept up with him much longer." I didn't know it then, but this was going to affect the outcome of the trial.

Many different people came and went during the court proceeding, and I didn't pay most of them any mind. The last day of the trial, I did notice an obese and poorly groomed woman milling about. She caught my attention because she only spoke with Leahey and never spoke with my attorney or me. At the end of the day, it was pointed out that she was Lisa Redmond, a reporter for the *Lowell Sun*.

The next day, Redmond published an article referring to me as "the defense" not the plaintiff. She characterized the Kennedy assault as a "tussle." Her article was extremely one-sided and fraught with false, misleading statements, such as, "Alvarez filed assault and battery charges against another officer. The case went nowhere." She didn't describe why it went nowhere, or discuss any of the lying that kept the case from going anywhere.

The article also stated that I claimed discrimination based solely on my Spanish surname, completely excluding the extensive evidence presented. She quoted Leahy as saying, "It was his superior attitude and his problems with leadership ... not his race, which have kept him achieving more within the department." Because she never spoke with myself or my attorney, we were not quoted.

She made no effort to find out all the aspects of the case. In the article, Redmond asked, "How can the chief allow him back on SWAT when he will not follow orders and thumbs his nose at everything over the past eight years?" Her article echoed Davis' lies and passed them off as the truth of the story. I was still a rogue with a bad attitude. She didn't even touch on the numerous lies that Davis and the others were caught in during the trial. Is that not newsworthy? This is my experience on how the *Lowell Sun* reports what they call news. In my opinion three police chiefs blatantly lying their asses off would take precedence in this story, but I'm not a reporter.

The jury deliberated for three days before coming back with its verdict. I needed twelve of the fourteen to agree in my favor on each element of the charges. Although most of the lying and incidents of disparate treatment were quite clear, you can never be sure if the jury sees things as clearly as everyone else. Still, when the verdict was handed to the judge, I felt confident. The jury had to be on my side, I thought. It saw several ranking police officials blatantly give false testimony, including three chiefs of police.

Judge Fishman held the verdict in his hands and began to read it quietly to himself before speaking. His facial expression turned to one of disgust as he looked over at the jury and just shook his head. He then read the verdict to the court with a distasteful tone. The jury found that I was in a protected class as a minority but they determined that there was no discrimination. I was just completely puzzled by this. We clearly presented all the elements of discrimination by law. The only way I thought I could lose this was if the jury agreed with the city and found that I was white; but it agreed that I was a minority of a protected class. What the hell was this?

My lawyer and I both anticipated that the jury would award a much higher amount than it did, based on what I had shown to have lost in wages and relentless stress during the trial. It awarded $60,000 in lost wages, $15,000 for emotional distress, and $90,000 in punitive damages for retaliation – a total of $165,000. This was significantly lower than what was demonstrated as my financial loss. I lost SWAT, which would have brought in $20,000 a year, and my executive protection career would have brought in $45,000 a year. That was $65,000 a year for nine years, and that was only some of my lost income. The $165,000 that I was awarded didn't come close to that.

Why was the amount so low? The jury believed that I failed to mitigate my damages. It came up with this idea all on its own. In a case where a person suffers damages incurred by someone or something else through no fault of his or her own, the courts believe that person should take reasonable steps to avoid further loss. How was I supposed to do that? The only way would have been to work extra details. The fact that I didn't was briefly touched upon when Leahy asked me why I didn't work extra details to make up the money I lost from my removal from SWAT and my specialty positions. I must not have explained it well enough, because the jury appeared to think that it was an option for me. Like everything else in the Lowell Police Department, the issuing of details favored some cops over others.

With how much they hated me, it was completely unrealistic that I ever would have been able to make up even a portion of what I lost. Lowell Police wouldn't let me use my vacation time, were they really going to give me overtime details?

After the end of the trial, I met the jurors in the lobby of the court house. They were all eager to speak to me as they gathered around us. They were overwhelmingly on my side, and understood that I had been through a lot. They asked if I was pleased at winning so much money. From their perspective, they thought they had awarded me a fortune. Based on the makeup of the jury, I think the jurors thought cops made too much money, and I know they thought that $165,000 was a lot. Compared to the $700k that I calculated as my loss; however, it really wasn't much at all.

They said they had struggled to come up with a determination for the amount for emotional distress because they felt I handled stress very well and showed no emotion when all the chiefs were lying and speaking badly about me. Maybe if I had cried like Kennedy, they would have found fit to award me something significant. They went on to say they were afraid to give me too much money because during the judge's jury directions they heard the judge say that he had the power to adjust the amount if he deemed it unreasonable. So they agreed on low figures so that it could not be taken away by the judge. The impression I got was that they were all disgusted at Davis, calling him a liar. One woman said, "We didn't think he was a racist, but we all thought he was an asshole."

I won my case in 2006, nine years after everything started. Davis and the city filed for an appeal, which we expected. I returned to work as usual, knowing that nothing would change. The award amount was so low that it didn't set off any alarms, and with the influence I felt Davis had over the local media, I knew the story was just going to get blown over.

Redmond was forced to write another article. This article plainly stated the amounts I had won and the verdict of each charge. Her article ended with this:

"He had alleged that due to his Spanish surname he was subject to discrimination. The city argued that Alvarez was passed over after a series of incidents allegedly involving a tussle with another cop and allegations of insubordination."

Once again, there was no mention of Davis and all the other police officers lying, nothing about them getting caught in their lies.

Due to interest, the $165k that I had been awarded was actually closer to $235k. The city filed for an appeal, knowing that this interest would continue to accrue. Marisa advised me that an appeal usually takes a couple of years. We had to just wait to see what legal points they planned to appeal on. As the years went by, Marisa assured me that it was a good thing became the interest was continuing to build; but after five years, it started getting ridiculous. Marisa made several attempts to coerce them into taking action, but they basically blew her off each time. Why wouldn't the city take any action to affect their appeal?

Davis and the city were well aware that I had attempted to have Davis criminally investigated for perjury from his testimony in his deposition. Davis had doubled down on his lying during the trial and he was caught in lies several times during his testimony. Previously the Massachusetts Attorney General was Bill O'Reilly, whose office would not investigate Davis. By the time my trial was over, we had a new Attorney General, Martha Coakley. I suspect Davis wasn't going to take the gamble that she wouldn't conduct an investigation. The statute of limitations for perjury is six years. After the six-year mark, the grounds for an investigation into the charges would be over. Until the case was officially concluded, which wouldn't happen until the appeal process was over, I couldn't file charges against Davis or any of the others for lying.

After Winning the Trial

When I returned to work, I was advised that there was an Internal Affairs investigation into the Geoffroy incident. Cullen, Shaw, and I were all interviewed by Captain Debbie Friedl and Lieutenant Jimmy Hodgdon. Davis was still in charge over all, although he was leaving to become the Police Commissioner in Boston soon and had begun to step back somewhat from his role in Lowell. Upon completion of their investigation, they exonerated Geoffroy of any wrongdoing and found that Shaw was in violation of "conduct unbecoming an officer," for spreading "vicious" rumors about Geoffroy. Because I didn't actually do anything, they couldn't punish me. Marisa filed the complaint to Taylor and not me, so I didn't violate my order to never file a complaint again. If I had, I would have been fired.

Throughout the years, as I pursued my case, I continued to take the sergeant's exam. After Kennedy was promoted, I stopped studying, and I only took the exam so I would have a score on the books. Davis had suspended me and the suspension was upheld by civil service, so I had no chance of getting promoted. Davis could always use the suspension as an excuse to bypass me no matter how high I scored.

I was hoping, as the civil case moved on, that the city might move to negotiate a deal to end everything. If I continued to take the exam, I would still have a score on the list. If the city chose to negotiate they could reach down on the sergeant list and make the promotion. I knew the city had done this with Otero and Fuller and, even though it was a less than zero chance for me, I took the test anyway.

In 2002 and 2004, I scored a 79 without any studying at all. After winning my case, I knew I had a real fighting chance to get promoted. If they bypassed my score because of the suspension that was still on my personnel file, it would be another legal fight, but I felt confident I could win this one. I just needed a high score. So I really hit the books hard, much harder than I did when I got an 85 several years earlier. When the scores came back, I found out that I received a 76, which was not a competitive score. Most city promotions were around 85 or higher.

I didn't stress out about it too much. At that point, my goal was to retire as soon as possible, my career as a police officer was essentially over. My focus turned away from law enforcement and I was now pursuing starting my own business and securing work as a military contractor in Afghanistan and Iraq. I had checked the retirement policy and I planned to put in my paper when I hit age 53. The score was the last thing on my mind.

Since then, I have puzzled over it some more. How did I get a 79 with absolutely no studying at all and then get the 76 score after seven months of diligent studying? Did I choke? I pondered long and hard over why I did so poorly after studying so painstakingly. Later, when I reflected on how Davis and the city surreptitiously undermined my career and my attempts to expose the corruption that existed there, I became suspicious.

First, my union assigned attorney sabotaged my chance to appeal my case to the Superior Court, where I clearly would have won. Second, my original MCAD complaint was dismissed and never investigated under the ridiculous assumption that I was not a minority. Third, my civil service file was deliberately tampered with and my race was changed to white from Hispanic, an incident that had never happened before. The race change only happened on the file of an officer with a racial discrimination case that was pending. This is beyond suspicious. Fourth, when the city finally filed its appeal for my case, it would be discovered that some of the court records of testimony from my trial were somehow missing. In over a century of the history of the court, no testimony had ever been lost, except for a trial where several police chiefs and officers committed perjury. Finally, in 1987, when I first became a cop, the biggest police story in the news was the Sergeant Exam scam. A Boston Police officer reported that he had stolen and sold copies of the civil service promotional exam. He had also tampered with rival officer's score sheets in order to lower their scores (Butterfield).

One basic rule of conducting an investigation is to acknowledge that there are no coincidences. If something appears like a coincidence, then there is probably something else going on and the investigator should examine it more closely. In this case, there is an abundance of coincidences. Everything combined does not look good, and I suspect that my exam and/or score may have been tampered with. I don't have proof, but all the evidence leads to a strong likelihood that this is what happened.

Maybe this isn't what happened, and I obviously will never know. There are other aspects of the test that have come under fire a number of times that could have been the reason behind my low score. It doesn't really make sense, but maybe it is something else.

Tests are not a good indicator of an officer's ability to do a good job. This is how the promotional testing system utilized in law enforcement is an intrinsic aspect of a system that creates incompetent and corrupt leadership. The exam has created a situation where skill and ability have nothing to do with getting promoted. Being politically connected and able to score well is all you need. Men like Kennedy might not do so well under pressure on the street, but they can score high on a test without even hardly trying. You have to have a mind for it, and Kennedy has that kind of mind. He beat everyone for the Lieutenant's Exam and the Captain's Exam, scoring higher than people who had years of experience in these roles and this helped him skyrocket up the ranks in Lowell.

When Davis left to become the Boston Police Commissioner, I thought everyone's need to suck up to Davis might ease a bit now that he was gone, and I looked forward to completing my career in Lowell on a more pleasant note. Everyone in the department knew I had never done any of the things I had been accused of, after all. Lavallee became the chief in Lowell, and I met with him and requested to return to SWAT and training.

At first, he told me there was nothing he could do because he was not the permanent superintendent, he was only there temporarily until it was determined who would take on the role permanently. Shortly thereafter, Lavallee was given the position officially, but he continued to stall.

"I need to speak to an attorney in the City law department. Once he tells me what to do, I will follow the instructions," he said.

Shortly thereafter, he appointed officers to the positions I had requested who were far less qualified and experienced than I was. I contacted my lawyer and we sent in a formal complaint to MCAD. They would hold it for two and a half years before dismissing it. From my experience, the MCAD is an absolute joke, if you want to get anything done, you have to hire an attorney and get the case pulled from MCAD to do a civil lawsuit. I believe it's a complete waste of taxpayer money.

Filing was enough to get some sort of reaction, though, at least this time. After filing my complaint, Deputy Arty Ryan called me into his office.

"Lavallee called me and said he will authorize your return to SWAT. You have to be a member of RRT (Rapid Response Team) for a year and then you will be allowed to tryout."

I was shocked. This was the last thing I expected. "No prior SWAT member has ever had to tryout or wait a year," I replied. "All prior SWAT members have been able to return without any requirements. It's always been that way."

"It's never been that way," he responded.

Ryan stared at me blankly, as if he didn't understand what I said, or he didn't care.

"I should be allowed to return to SWAT immediately without a tryout like everyone else. That's how it's always been," I reiterated.

Ryan sighed. "Right, well, I don't know anything about that. But your prior experience doesn't count. You have to do RRT for a year first and then tryout, just like everyone else."

"So I'm the only one whose experience doesn't count?" I barked.

"Based on my tactical experience, these are the rules for everyone and it has always been this way. You are asking for special treatment, and you're not going to get it. Just take this as a 'gift' and don't make waves. Stop being angry and accept the situation for what it is."

Ryan knew this was a lie, but as an officer with rank he had the ability to say anything he wanted and there wasn't much I could do about it at that moment. This is one of those unwritten rules you learn about after you become a cop. Ryan had never been on SWAT, he had no tactical experience with the team. But again, rank gets to supersede the truth. Also, Ryan was mad because during the trial, it was presented that he committed an indecent sexual assault of a female employee. He grabbed a woman's breast at a department Christmas party and asked her if it was real. The woman filed a complaint, but later dropped it, and there were rumors that the city paid her off. There was no investigation and Ryan never received punishment. He eventually got promoted to deputy chief. Marisa and I tried to introduce it as evidence in order to show instances of disparate treatment. Judge Fishman wouldn't allow it, though, because examples of disparate treatment had to be similar acts. I was accused of being a danger to other officers, Ryan just grabbed some woman's breasts.

Presently, an officer has to join the RRT and participate there for a year before he is allowed to join SWAT. Once a person is on SWAT, if he leaves for a while and comes back, there is no need to tryout again. The officer was brought back on the team without any prerequisite. I knew this because I had actually left SWAT for a few years while I was working in Waltham because that department wasn't a member of NEMLEC at the time that I worked there. When I transferred to Lowell, I was immediately allowed to return to SWAT at Roarke's request. Consequently, I should have been able to return to the team immediately without issue; requiring me to join RRT for a year and then tryout again was ridiculous.

The tryout requirement was especially insulting. The SWAT Team was created in 1986 and I came on the team in 1988 when I was a police officer in Groton. George Thistle and I came on together, and we were both in outstanding shape. Frank Roarke was in charge and he came up with the first set of tryouts for us. It involved a number of calisthenics, followed by an obstacle course and then a mile run with full gear, weapons, and ammo while wearing a gas mask. The run finished at the range, where you immediately shot the stress handgun shooting course of fire for time. Our times on the course became the standard to meet. My score on the stress handgun course was 99 out of a possible hundred. I had one bullet just outside the line. Buddie Fuller scored a 98 a few years later. Our scores were the highest score recorded for years. It's unknown if they were ever surpassed. For me, the tryout would be a walk in the park, but I shouldn't have had to do it to get back on the team.

After speaking with Ryan, I called Paul Cooper because he had replaced Roarke as the head of SWAT. Ryan's statements were absurd. Cooper knew who I was and the quality of my work, I figured he could get things straightened out.

"Hey, Coop," I said when he picked up the phone. "I just got the word that I can return to the team, but Ryan is telling me I have to tryout first. Can you straighten this out for me?"

"Mm," Cooper grunted a response.

"Well, no one has ever had to do that before, you know this, right?"

"Uh..." He wasn't really saying much, so I kept going. For some reason, he was unable to speak in full sentences.

"Look, I know there's tryouts this week, do you want me to go?"

"Mm. Uh," he grunted again.

"Coop, do you want me to tryout, or do you want me to go to RRT?"

"Go to RRT."

"Okay," I said, wondering why he was acting so weird. "What about my equipment? Is NEMLEC issuing it still or is it issued by the home departments now?"

"Hm, well, uh, uh, I got to go." That was the end of the conversation. He would never have the guts to speak to me again. That was the last conversation I would even have with him either on the phone or face to face.

After that, I went to the uniform shop to get my uniform for RRT. I told them to put the RRT and SWAT patches on my uniform as all prior members wore the SWAT patch. The badges and patches were like uniform badges in the military, once you've earned them, you wore them forever. The girl at the shop handed me my uniform and I looked it over.

"Where's my SWAT patch?" I asked her.

"Oh, well, Sergeant Cooper said not to put them on. He says you're not going to get on SWAT anyway, and you don't rate the patch."

This is how I found out they weren't going to put me back on SWAT. It was clear to me that Paul Cooper, the SWAT Team commander, didn't have the balls to say it to me to my face. What a pussy. This was my experience with the quality of leadership of the SWAT command personnel, especially after I came back. This is how cops work. Everything is behind your back. Never look a man in the eye.

I called my attorney.

"Looks like I've got to put you back to work," I sighed. I really thought this whole thing was going to be over after I won my case.

I shouldn't have been surprised that Cooper didn't have the guts to tell me I wasn't on SWAT. When I had been on the team previously, Cooper was basically an equipment guy, he never held any position of authority. Officially, he was a sniper, but we never deployed snipers on SWAT operations, so he mostly drove the van.

I had always pushed to deploy the snipers on operations, even if we weren't going to use them, for actual experience and training purposes. Setting up in training is different from setting up in the city where our operations were. I believed that they needed to go out with us, so they could build actual operational experience, and practice finding the best place to observe and gather intelligence. They needed this. With most of these operations, you don't need to set up the snipers, but let's get them actually operational in the environment where they might have to take a shot. That's what I was pushing for, but then I was removed and the issue died. This is an example of me being the "independent thinker" that Silva testified to, that supposedly made him question my obedience. If I had stayed on, I would have pushed for it more, and maybe it would have changed. The snipers never really got any field experience and when I returned to the team their training had lapsed even more under Cooper.

Before I was removed, we had an operation with a barricaded gunman who was drunk and wanted to kill himself along with everyone else. I had been the team leader on a number of operations, and when the van pulled up to the Billerica Police station, I was in the front passenger seat and Cooper was driving. Silva, who was the commander of the SWAT/RRT team, stepped to the driver's door and asked Cooper to be in charge and set up the team. Cooper was clearly shocked because he had never done it before, it was usually my job. I was sitting next to Cooper, and Silva just ignored me.

I didn't do or say anything for the whole drive to the scene, but I kept looking over at Cooper. He seemed to be in shock, and he never gave any directions to the team. I kept looking at him, waiting for him to take command, but he didn't. We got to the house and he still hadn't issued any orders. It couldn't wait any longer. We were there and we had a guy who was armed and barricaded. We had to move.

"Give me two shield men!" I yelled, and two guys jumped out the back. I grabbed another guy, Timmy McDonough. McDonough had been on the team a few years, but this was his first time he would be on the entry team. I had a team of four and headed into the inner perimeter while Cooper stayed with the van.

"I'm just a sniper anyway," he said. He seemed happy that I took over.

This was an operation where we really broke from standard procedures. It was late at night and the gunman was really drunk and started to nod off while the negotiator was trying to maintain a conversation with him. The negotiator kept calling out to him down the hall, but he stopped answering and he could be heard snoring off and on.

"The guy sounds pretty out of it," Roarke told me. "I think you can sneak down the hall and jump him before he wakes up."

"Let's wait a few more minutes to make sure he's really out," I reluctantly agreed.

Prior to our arrival, this guy had already fired a couple of rounds from his 30/30 Winchester lever action rifle that ripped through the house, so we knew he wasn't afraid to shoot. In retrospect, sneaking down the hall to tackle him wasn't the best or safest idea. We dumped the ballistic shields because the rifle round would have gone right through them anyway. We lined up, first with Tony Morlani who had empty hands so he could grab the guy, then me with my pistol drawn as the designated shooter, and behind us were Mike "OT" O'Toole and McDonough. The four of us started tip toeing down the hallway to the bedroom.

We had actually used this sneak up while they are sleeping tactic before two years earlier with a homicidal man with a gun, but the situation was different. Last time the gunman actually had no clue the police were coming into his home and we had complete and total surprise on our side. I was the first man with my handgun out and the second man was Jimmy Cormier with empty hands. That time it all worked as planned, but it was risky, and when we debriefed we all decided it wasn't something we should do again. Yet here we were, doing it again, this time without the element of surprise. Even knowing what was on the line, it was amazing how silent we were. We were loaded down with gear in a tiny hallway, but you could hardly even hear anyone breathing. If this guy woke up before we could jump him, it was going to be a deadly, close up, and personal gun fight.

Tony and I entered the room to see a large, middle-aged man in his underwear, half sitting up against the headboard. The rifle lay across his chest and his finger was on the trigger. When we crept up to the foot of the bed, he opened his eyes. In a split second, Tony jumped on him and pinned his rifle down as I jammed the muzzle of my pistol into his eye socket.

I found this tactic to be very effective in the past, because the person immediately loses partial vision and experiences abrupt distracting pain. If I had to take the shot, it would shut him down instantly and it would not put anyone else in the struggle in danger of being hit. In most any other case I would never make body contact with my muzzle. Because the eyeball is soft, when you push the muzzle into the eye, the pistol won't go out of battery. With a pistol, if you place the barrel against something, like any other body part and push, you can make the slide move back and take the gun out of battery. I never needed to fire though, OT and McDonough piled on quickly, and the guy never knew what hit him. The operation was completed and no one got hurt. This was my last operation before my removal from SWAT.

After the woman at the uniform store told me I wasn't getting on SWAT, I went to the RRT training instead of SWAT training where the tryout was being held. Billy MacKenzie had replaced Silva as the SWAT/RRT commander. When I got there, I pulled him aside to talk to him.

"What's going on, why am I not being allowed back on the team?"

"You're a danger to the team, Bob. Stanley, Ryan, and I decided that it's been too long since you've been on the team, and your return is a liability and a safety issue. You can't tryout today. You need to get indoctrinated through RRT for a year and tryout again."

"What do you mean I'm a danger to the team?"

"Look, your past experience on SWAT makes you a safety issue. I don't want any problems with you," he said.

"I have never been a problem, and I've never caused any problems either. What's this all about?"

"I just don't want any problems with you," he repeated. "I don't want to know about your fucking lawsuit and I don't care."

McKenzie continued. "I want to let you know, too, that if I get any pressure from above to change your status, I will fight it. I will do anything I can to keep you off my team and to keep my team safe."

With that, I walked away. This was an interesting twist. Before my experience didn't count, and now my experience made me dangerous? There was another guy, Junior Doherty, who was on the team, who accidentally shot himself while he was in the police station. He was also an admitted alcoholic with numerous disciplinary issues on his record. He wasn't a danger or a liability, but I was?

To add insult to injury, McKenzie had been a SWAT team member for approximately the same number of years I had. He left the team and was absent for nine years, which was about the same amount of time that I had been gone. He was allowed to return without question. Not only was he allowed back on the team without a tryout, he was also given the position of Commander. So now he was in charge and believed he could make up his own rules and say whatever he wanted. I hope by this time you can see that there is a distinct pattern with these guys who reach high levels of authority. How was I any different other than the fact that I was a minority? The only minority that was ever on the team.

Marisa contacted NEMLEC and pointed out the blatant disparate treatment and advised that a civil lawsuit would follow if they failed to correct their conduct. She laid out the elements of discrimination and discussed Cooper's cowardly conduct. She pointed to documentation showing that prior members were allowed to return with no questions raised. Cooper himself had been removed from the team and returned some years later with no restrictions.

As far the argument about my return being a safety issue, it was pointed out that I had actually saved the life of another team member and that I had been in several use-of-force encounters where I refrained from using deadly force. She compared my performance with that of Doherty, who had been removed from the team and allowed to return on several occasions without incident in spite of being a drunk who shot himself.

The issue of experience was also addressed. The claim that my SWAT experience made me a danger was beyond idiotic and we decided not to respond to it. The claim about how my experience didn't count was then compared with the fact that Lowell had allowed two other officers, Dave Frechette and Jason Nobrego to join the team when they had no SWAT experience at the time. So what was NEMLEC's defense for these two contrasting positions other than discrimination?

Shortly thereafter, I was invited to return to the team. Apparently the NEMLEC chiefs addressed Cooper's conduct concerning the uniform shop and he immediately quit the SWAT Team. The day I got back on the team they announced Cooper's resignation. The guys clearly held me responsible for Cooper quitting, with most of them giving me the cold shoulder from day one. Even the guys I had trained and worked with in the past wouldn't talk to me.

I made Kennedy cry, I hurt the trooper's feelings, and I made Cooper quit. None of them were responsible for their own actions, it was always my fault.

Getting back on SWAT wasn't what I had expected at all. It was a very adversarial environment. I thought that because these guys knew me and they knew my skill level, if I gave it some time they would come around, but they never did. They did reveal who they really were, though. After that, I held them all in complete contempt. They were all totally disgraceful in my eyes. In the past, I would not have hesitated to put my life on the line for any of them, and now I knew that level of commitment was not shared by them.

Sometime before the trial, I ran into Harry Sawyer, a Burlington cop and SWAT member who I had trained in the past. He expressed he was clearly on my side and told me straight out he would testify on my behalf if needed. As the trial progressed and I was blindsided with all the lying, I called Sawyer to take him up on his offer. I wanted his testimony to counter Crowley and the chief's testimony. Sawyer responded that he wouldn't be able to help me. I don't know what changed. I wouldn't have called him if he hadn't offered, and this was an unexpected response.

Timmy McDonough is also a Burlington cop and is now a sergeant in charge of their drug unit. Apparently he didn't like the fact that I asked Sawyer to testify in my case. With the team blaming me for making Cooper quit, McDonough felt emboldened to call me out.

"You called Harry and wanted him to testify in your lawsuit," he said in front of the team one day. "You're an ass."

God forbid you ask a cop to testify to the truth on the stand.

I couldn't believe McDonough was calling me out on this. I gave him his first assignment on a SWAT contact team to take out that barricaded gunman in Billerica. He was a timid kid who originally was terrified to rappel. I was the rappel master in the tower and I really had to coddle him because of his fear of heights. Now he had actually been on SWAT longer than me and had rank above me. It must have been a great ego boost to shit on me in front of the team. His attitude is the status quo if you want to move up, which he has.

Dave Frechette had just been promoted to sergeant and he was following the Lowell tradition of saying whatever he wanted whether or not it was true. He was offended that I used the fact that he and Nobrega had no SWAT experience prior to joining SWAT as my defense to get back on the team. He also called me out in front of the team, claiming that I had stated he wasn't qualified to be on SWAT and that he had seen this in the court transcripts of my case. This took me completely off guard. It was especially remarkable because I never talked about Frechette and Nobrega in my trial, so the information would not have been in the transcripts. Not to mention the fact that I couldn't get copies of the transcripts myself. It was pretty amazing how he twisted this around; he felt victimized by my discrimination case. My case was about the discrimination I had to tolerate at the hands of NEMLEC personnel, but somehow he felt my case was about him.

His attitude was completely in keeping with everything I had observed with police supervisors. The higher in rank individuals rose, the more self-centered their perceptions became. This supreme self-centered narcissism was displayed in Davis' demand for my total loyalty to him in the face of his appalling treatment of me. My ideology of supervision and leadership were on a drastically different plane. When I was moving up the ranks in the Marines from fire team leader, to squad leader, to platoon sergeant, I never once felt it was about me. I felt my job was to serve the men of my platoon. They came first and I was dedicated to their success, not mine. This mindset created a mutual respect and brotherhood that has lasted a lifetime. Many of the men who served under me are still my closest friends today.

I also had a younger, newer kid on the SWAT team inform me that this just wasn't a team, "they were a family," of which I was not included. I don't remember this kid's name other that he was from a small-town department. They want to talk about family. I'm quite sure that I'm the only SWAT member to have another team member live with him. Ronnie LeBlanc, a sergeant from the Wakefield Police Department and his wife, moved into my house when they sold their old house and were waiting for the build of their new home to be completed.

At some point after I was removed from SWAT and MacKenzie took over, LeBlanc was in a situation where he wasn't capable of maintaining the physical standards of the team anymore. He was allowed to stay on in spite of this because of his experience. With the team turning its back on me, LeBlanc followed suit. Even guys I had been close to before were giving me the cold shoulder.

I had asked LeBlanc to testify for me during my case, thinking he would want to help out a friend. Although he didn't say no, I never heard from him again. After my case concluded, I continued to stay abreast of civil service promotional cases because I knew I would have to fight if I ever got the chance to be promoted again. While I was conducting my own research, I came upon case # G-2456, Brown vs.Town of Wakefield, decided April 20, 1994. Brown, with a score of 87, was bypassed for LeBlanc, who only scored an 83. The police department promoted LeBlanc to sergeant and Brown filed his case with civil service for bypassing him.

The city's response for promoting LeBlanc over Brown was as follows: LeBlanc was a firearms and OC spray instructor. He had received specialized training while a NEMLEC member of RRT and SWAT. It was emphasized that this was extra work done on a voluntary basis above and beyond what is required from an officer. It was pointed out that he was a sergeant 1st class of the National Guard, Finance Battalion, and had received an excellent rating on his fitness reports. He had also been on a security team for U.S. officials. Civil service upheld Leblanc's bypass promotion based on his extensive experience over Brown.

Like Brown, Kennedy had no specialized skill. Kennedy's score was 86; my score was 85. LeBlanc received training on RRT and SWAT; I was an instructor on RRT and SWAT. LeBlanc's National Guard fitness report rating was "excellent." My Marine Corps fitness report rating as a platoon sergeant was "outstanding," which is better than excellent. My work in the executive protection field also included protection of high ranking U.S. officials. The Wakefield chief promoted Leblanc, Davis chose to promote Kennedy. The Brown vs. Wakefield case would have been a huge boost during my trial, if I had only known about it. Because I considered Leblanc a friend; he was well informed on my situation, my score, and my case. His case could have significantly affected the outcome of my case, yet he chose to remain silent. He could have at least told me about the case, his testimony wasn't even really necessary in this case. To me, this silence reflected not only his inability to stand up for a friend and fellow officer, but also demonstrated a level of fear and cowardice that I will never understand.

With Cooper gone, the SWAT Team Command went to Steve Chaput, who came on the team a few years after me. Based on my observations of him, his performance could be deemed average at best. He was a minion of Crowley's back in the day, and you rarely saw one without the other. Like Crowley, Chaput was often missing from operations. He never held a leadership position, nor was he ever an instructor of any discipline. He was from a small town police department in Dracut and was now a Lieutenant, and he had been on the team roster for 17 years. Obviously this qualified him to command the team.

In the early days, the leadership consisted of mostly men with a lot of military qualifications. Frank Roarke was prior Army Special Forces, and he was airborne and scuba qualified. Larry Reading was also prior Army Special Forces, a Vietnam vet, and he was airborne qualified. Mackenzie was a Vietnam vet and airborne qualified. I was prior Marines, and airborne and scuba qualified. We all wore our qualifications badges on our camouflage utility uniforms.

On my first day back, Mackenzie came up to me and pointed at my jump wings and scuba badge. "We don't wear those here."

"Since when?" I asked. Then I looked closer at his uniform. "You're wearing your jump wings tab," I retorted. Then I just walked away from him.

At the end of the day, Chaput approached me. "MacKenzie wants you to take the jump wings and scuba badge off. You know you really need to be qualified to wear them anyway."

"No shit, Stevie, you know I'm qualified." I said, exasperated.

"Well, you're wearing badges and Mackenzie is wearing a tab. MacKenzie says your badges are a safety issue, can you take them off?"

I sighed. "Fine."

I remember hearing Roarke and Larry Redding referring to MacKenzie as an "idiot." I had been on a number of operations with him before he left the team, but hadn't come to the same conclusion until my return. It appears once you make rank, you feel more free to voice your bigotry.

In actuality, there were a couple of guys on the team who had been Army Rangers and they did not wear any qual badges, so I didn't mind taking them off. But MacKenzie still wore his, and being accused once again that I wasn't qualified pissed me off. Again, what was this safety issue thing? Everything with me was a "safety issue." I was removed from SWAT because I was a danger to other police officers, "a safety issue." My SWAT experience was considered a "safety issue." My military qualification badges, which few Americans rate to wear, was a "safety issue."

The training conducted in the eighties and nineties by Roarke and Redding was quality training. In these early days of SWAT, there weren't any national standards, so we were learning as we moved along. The training was adequate for what we had experienced in operations so far. When Roarke felt confident with the team's operational abilities, he focused on competing at the SWAT Roundup in Florida. A lot of our training time was devoted to competition shooting in preparation for the Roundup. I followed orders and competed, but I felt we should have been working on skill building for actual events that we may find ourselves facing.

Back in the day, we pioneered our own training regimen, which was based on our military experience coupled with direct knowledge gained from actual operations. When I started with SWAT, the National Tactical Officers Association (NTOA) was just being established and I became the 43rd member. The association grew over the years and has over 40,000 members now. It provides education and training support for SWAT, and develops standard operational procedures (SOP) that have become readily accepted nationwide.

When Roarke allowed me to conduct training, my goal was to introduce more decision shooting, night shooting, chemical environment shooting, and team movement, coupled with decision shooting coupled with tactical deployment of smoke and distraction devices. I wanted to add skills built upon these foundations, incorporating the tactical use of the ballistic shield and the ballistic shield two-man team concept. I wanted us to feel confident with our abilities to go into a worst-case scenario. We needed to be able to go into a totally chaotic incident of mass casualties, hostage situation with multiple skilled active shooters and not say, "Oh shit." My intention was to train up to the level where we could go head long into incidents like the recent Paris terrorist events without missing a beat. I thought we could achieve this level in a few years or so, but I was removed a couple of months into my plan.

Upon my return, I found out that the team rarely went to the shooting range under Cooper and the ballistic shield had been basically dropped as a tool and there was no training with it. For a team that had been around over twenty years, it should have surpassed these goals years ago. In my mind, training needed to be addressed immediately.

When Chaput first took over the team, these things didn't concern him as much as they did me. Chaput's first e-mails to the SWAT Team as their new commander did not address training at all. One evening shift, I was on a department computer and opened my inbox to discover an e-mail that had been sent to SWAT Team members from him titled, "Kidnap Plot Foiled" (S. Chaput, personal communication, October 27, 2008). The e-mail contained a photo of a box held up by a stick with a watermelon under the box. Barack Obama has just become the presidential nominee and he was obviously the subject of the e-mail.

Sometime after receiving this correspondence, the team received another e-mail, this time after Obama was elected, titled "Inauguration Practice" (S. Chaput, personal communication, December 19, 2008). This e-mail contained a video of a black man dancing around in a grass skirt in an African village while "Moving on Up," the theme song from *The Jeffersons* played in the background. Both emails were also addressed to Mackenzie, who was the overall commander of SWAT and RRT. Clearly racist jokes were his priority, not training deficits. This was the guy who was running SWAT now.

He never got in any trouble for it either. There were stories of other cops doing similar things around the country when Obama was elected, and they were all fired or demoted (Munsi). On the NEMLEC SWAT team, however, it was completely acceptable.

With Chaput in charge, the team did start training at the shooting range more frequently, but the shooting was focused on more basic individual marksmanship skills, which is just a step up from regular police firearms qualifications. The weapons discipline, or lack thereof, was nothing I would have tolerated in the past or in the Marine Corps. Also, the way training was run was completely different from in the past. There was so much down time and so much standing around talking, that only two hours of actual training occurred out of an eight-hour training day on SWAT training days.

We also trained eight hours a month with RRT. Back when I was running training, we trained four hours with RRT, and the last four hours were SWAT training time. Roarke had granted this training time to me to run and I had the team go directly to the shooting range. Now that I was back, after RRT training was over, the SWAT team met in a conference room and basically held a bullshit session. We got four hours of overtime for SWAT training and we were just sitting around. This was something Cooper instilled and Chaput saw fit to carry on with it. This was standard procedure at least until I retired in 2010.

Davis Appointed as Commissioner of Boston Police

In 2006, shortly after my court case was concluded, Davis became the Police Commissioner in Boston, Massachusetts. His appointment to this position was largely based on two things. One was the reports that he had lowered crime by 60% during his time working in Lowell (or was it 50%? 42%? Again, we will never really know). Davis had been praised by the *Lowell Sun* for making Lowell one of the nation's safest communities, and this praise for his ability to reduce crime made him a top candidate for Commissioner. Another thing working in his favor was the work he had done training officers across the country in "race relations, ethics and integrity" (Estes). By now, I have shown how none of these things were actually true and that Davis was not actually qualified for the position or to be a police officer at all.

Because Davis' success in Lowell was based on a made-up statistic that was backed up by a combination of manipulating records, doubling the police force of the city, and good timing; he was criticized for being unable to replicate his astounding results in Boston (Cramer). In fact, the clearance rate of homicides in Boston decreased during the first two years of his tenure, despite his efforts to increase the size of the homicide unit in Boston.

Additionally, Davis continued to treat the minority officers in his department differently from the white officers. While in Boston, there are numerous examples of ways minority officers have received different treatment from white officers under his leadership. A few of these follow:

A white officer was accused of using excessive force and making up reports and testimony. This officer was given a five-working-day suspension with two days to serve. A black officer was terminated for being accused of using excessive force. Meanwhile, remember how Davis allowed the city of Lowell to pay out thousands of dollars in lawsuits for an officer who consistently used excessive force?

A white officer was arrested for assault after getting into a bar fight and she was given a ten-working-day suspension with four days to serve. A black officer was accused of assault and battery, but the charges were not sustained. Her punishment? A one-year suspension with five months to serve, the balance was suspended, and she was placed on lifetime probation.

Another white officer was arrested for assault and placed on supervised probation. Punishment? Thirty days suspension with five days to serve. A black officer arrested for assault but found not guilty received forty-five days of suspension with fifteen days to serve (Community Forum Leadership of the Boston Police Department).

Clearly the punishment meted out to officers of color differs wildly from punishments doled out to white officers. While Davis may have been able to get away with this type of behavior for years in Lowell, it wasn't long before people in Boston noticed and began to call for something to change.

In 2011, the city of Lowell finally presented its case to the appeals court. As it prepared its case, it was discovered that records of witness testimony had somehow gone missing. With missing testimony, the city believed its appeal would be hampered and it requested a new trial. The clerk of court reported that in the history of Cambridge Superior Court, there had never been a case where court testimony was ever lost. It appears a strange coincidence that the only case that ever had lost testimony was a case that contained several chiefs and police officers committing perjury. The court overlooked this hardship and denied the city's request for a new trial because the city stalled its appeal for so long and it was reaching the six-year mark. The court instructed the city to move forward with presenting its appeal.

The appeals court was the only authority openly to acknowledge Davis' lying in all the years that I fought to have justice served (Appeals Court Finding, P. 5-6). It was the only organization that recognized his behavior as inappropriate. It was frustrating, but also a relief to have my experience finally validated. I am going to quote extensively from this document because the wording used is a strong testament to the truth of my case and the acts of perjury I faced while taking Davis and Lowell to court. If the reader is interested in reading this document directly, it can be found online (Appeals Court Finding, Alvarez vs. Lowell).

The document begins by summarizing the evidence presented in my case. It discusses my career, and the many achievements I had accrued before coming to Lowell and in my first years there. It then summarized instances of discrimination and retaliation that I experienced while working in Lowell.

It then goes into the three incidents that Davis used as his reasons for removing me from my special positions. In response to the state police incident, the appeals court said that the "evidence was flatly contradicted" (Appeals Court Finding, Alvarez vs. Lowell, P. 5). It said the same thing about the SWAT incident, that Davis' testimony was “flatly contradicted” (Appeals Court Finding, Alvarez vs. Lowell, P. 6). The court went even further by saying that “without any evidence of any kind ... Davis unfairly and incorrectly assumed that Alvarez was at the center of these actions” (Appeals Court Finding, Alvarez vs. Lowell, P. 5) when discussing the events surrounding Marchionda’s funeral. Again, it repeats that Davis had “no evidence to support his wild assertions” (Appeals Court Finding, Alvarez vs. Lowell, P. 6). Let that sink in for a minute. A court of law said Davis’ claims were wild assertions. Pretty strong accusation for a man who has risen to national prominence for his role in an event that deeply affected our nation.

Next, the appeals court addressed the Kennedy incident by stating that my decision to correct Kennedy was appropriate. It acknowledged that the conflicting reports from the evening (due to everyone lying on the stand but not collaborating to make sure their lies matched up) made it difficult to determine exactly what happened. Still, it acknowledged that “Alvarez has been punished for nine years, in sharp contrast, Kennedy made a meteoric rise in the LPD” (Appeals Court Finding, Alvarez vs. Lowell, P. 8). It then pointed out that Davis claimed he used reports that didn’t exist to make his decision to suspend me and that his testimony concerning the events of that evening did not match the reports to which he had access.

Other than Davis, the only person recognized by the appeals court as lying was Demoura, which was disappointing to me.

Next, the court delves into the other claims made by Davis for his reasons to consistently deny my requests to get these positions back. The court mentioned that there were numerous supervisors who testified that I was never disrespectful. It acknowledged that Otero also was subjected to adverse treatment at the hands of Davis.

The court stated that it was "odd" that Davis appointed me to train new officers and never sent me to any sort of psychological counseling, in spite of his claims that my attitude never changed.

The summary ends by stating that "Alvarez offered substantial and detailed testimony regarding his damages including the lost income" (Appeals Court Finding, Alvarez vs. Lowell, P. 15) from my lost positions.

The appeals court finding then explores the arguments presented by the city. The first was in regard to the sufficiency of the evidence presented in court, the second was a contestation of the damages awarded to me, and then there were several appeals on technicalities.

The courts start by stating that the "reasonableness of Alvarez's beliefs and actions were questions of fact for the jury to decide" (Appeals Court Finding, Alvarez vs. Lowell, P. 15). I provided plenty of evidence of wrongful discrimination as well as "evidence showing serious inaccuracies in the city's investigations and accounts" (Appeals Court Finding, Alvarez vs. Lowell, P. 15) of the incidents. The argument that I was emotionally unstable was not supported by evidence. The city's reasons for the disparate treatment were "flimsy at best" (Appeals Court Finding, Alvarez vs. Lowell, P. 16). It added that the privileges and promotions enjoyed by Kennedy after the incident between the two of us also supported my argument that I had been discriminated against.

The appeals court finalized things by stating that the city gave "inaccurate and misleading information" (Appeals Court Finding, Alvarez vs. Lowell, P. 16) in my MCAD case, and then discussed the numerous positions and privileges that I was denied thereafter. The court ultimately ruled that the findings of the jury was supported by the evidence. Appeal denied.

As far as the damages were concerned, the court found that the argument that the compensatory amount awarded to me was too high because the judge did not give proper instructions was invalid. The evidence fully supported the emotional distress damages that I was awarded. The punitive damages were also supported because the "reliance on inaccurate and misleading information" by Davis and his men was behavior that "called for condemnation and deterrence" (Appeals Court Finding, Alvarez vs. Lowell, P. 17).

The court concludes by saying that all of the arguments on technicalities are invalid.

So, basically, the city had absolutely no logical grounds to appeal yet knowing this it stalled the appeal for six years, even as the case accrued approximately $120 a day to be paid by the taxpayers of Lowell. Why wait six years? Because the statute of limitations for the crime of perjury is six years, and this action protected Davis, the other chiefs, and all the other command staff from criminal investigation and prosecution. The city and Davis were rightfully aware I would pursue a criminal investigation of all the lying and false testimony by all of the police officials in this trial. Clearly the city solicitor, city manager, and mayor all agreed their best course of action was to support the corruption of Davis and these several police officers. These politicians had no vested interest in supporting criminal activity and corruption, but they chose to abandon any level of justice, truth, or integrity and preserve and protect the careers of these dirty cops. The truth was just too messy and this type of truth would tarnish the city's reputation. Even after all these years, I cannot escape my feelings of amazement and disgust at their conduct.

Marisa calculated the total amount due was approximately $600,000 and allowed the city law office time to make budget adjustments to accommodate the payout. The city made an initial payment of $120,000 with the understanding that the balance would be paid after the fiscal budget plan was approved the following year. I had no problem with this because it would increase the payment by an additional $44,000. After the time had lapsed and the city had its new annual budget, Marisa called the city's law office and spoke with the city solicitor, Christine O'Connor. O'Connor told Marisa that by accepting the $120,000 earlier, the city was free of its obligation to pay the rest and that Marisa had "verbally forfeited" any future payment. Marisa responded with a myriad of politely put legal facts that demonstrated O'Connor's moronic position, after which no one at the city's law office would return Marisa's phone call or e-mails. This shows what type of attorney the City of Lowell has working for it.

After some time, Marisa attempted to call the *Lowell Sun,* but it, too, was unresponsive. Legally, the city had to pay us, but it quickly became obvious that it wasn't going to be easy getting the city to follow up on its obligation. Marisa maintained her barrage of calls and emails for several weeks until finally O'Connor came to the conclusion that we were not going away. On September 13, 2013, O'Connor finally relented, and agreed to pay the balance in full. Marisa drove up to Lowell from Boston and demanded the check in person.

In April 2013, the Boston Marathon Bombing occurred. Davis became the media mouthpiece for the police during this event because he was the commissioner when everything went down. The media painted him as a hero for all the work he did to find the bombers. There truly was an abundance of heroic acts by first responders to save the lives of all the injured and amputee victims. Everyone present pulled together and got all the wounded transported to the hospital. It's an amazing feat that everyone transported to the hospital survived. The investigation conducted by the FBI and BPD quickly identified the suspects. The processing of the crime scene and utilization of video surveillance was exemplary. The heroic conduct of all the people involved should be recognized and applauded.

But crediting the bulk of this heroism on the shoulders of Davis is a drastic misplacement. Davis' primary role in the incident was to go on television and talk about what the police were doing. Davis is well versed in addressing fear of crime and he was successful projecting confidence on camera. This event catapulted him onto the national stage.

On August 1, 2013, approximately a month before the city paid out on my lawsuit, news articles started to appear reporting that Davis was on the short list for the Homeland Security Director's position (Sacchetti). I was greatly alarmed by this. How could someone so corrupt, whose career in law enforcement was a complete lie, reach this level?

Then that same week, on August 7, 2013, the newspapers printed an article titled, "Minority Officers Call for Edward Davis's Resignation" (Anderson). The article stated that members of the Massachusetts Association of Minority Law Enforcement Officers (MAMLEO) were reporting widespread incidents of discrimination occurring under Davis' leadership. I felt compelled to get my story out, the American public needed to know the truth. Knowing that Davis had continued to discriminate against minorities and that he continued to behave the way he had in Lowell was all the encouragement I needed. I needed to save the country from having Davis reach the Homeland Security position. I sent e-mails to all three major news television stations in Boston: WBZ channel 4, WCVB channel 5, and WHDH channel 7. None of them responded.

I distinctly took note of a *Boston Globe* article dated January 2010 entitled, "Officers Who Lie will be Dismissed," where it was reported that Davis announced he would fire any officer who lied in any proceeding. This was the apex of hypocrisy. While commissioner in Boston, Davis vowed to uphold a zero-tolerance policy for officers who were caught lying while in the line of duty. He proposed this policy in response to a scandal that involved a Boston police officer who was sentenced to 26 years in prison for charges relating to a sex and drug den that he ran. Several officers were involved, and either went to jail or received discipline for lying and drug use. Davis' proposed policy would allow him to fire any cop caught lying in the line of duty, after an Internal Affairs investigation, of course.

This proposal was lauded for being the strictest policy of its kind in the nation (Fargen). It was also criticized by some because the idea of police policing themselves is worrisome. Critics believed the actions of an officer caught lying should be reviewed by a civilian board, not one run by the police (Nadeau). Knowing Davis' track record, I feel that leaving any decision that could permanently affect an officer's career in the hands of Internal Affairs is probably not the best idea. Furthermore, with his history of lying and especially committing perjury, it was a ridiculously hypocritical position for him to take.

The article that caught my eye was written by John Ellement, and I thought for sure he would show some interest in my story. I sent him a detailed e-mail and followed up with a phone call a few days later. I spoke with Ellement over the phone and he said he had received my e-mail. When I asked if he was interested in running the story, he responded that he didn't know yet, and that someone would get back to me. I never heard from him or anyone from the *Globe* again. I later saw a news article in the *Boston Globe* announcing that a number of their writers were working on a book deal to write about the Marathon Bombing (Unknown, 2013). Would exposing Davis affect their book deals? Could this be why they refused to take on my story?

When no one in the news media would cover the story of my lawsuit, I sent an e-mail to MAMLEO. Its response was immediate. Upon its request, I sent it the Appeals Court finding of my case (Robert Alvarez vs. the City of Lowell). This court document was then posted on the Boston Police Superior Officer's Federation website for all 2,300 officers in Boston and the public to read.

On September 12, 2013, the day after the posting on this website, I received a phone call from Jimmy Myers, a radio talk show host from Touch 106.1 FM, which broadcasts out of Boston. Jimmy Myers began speaking about my case on his show. He read the letters from Bob and Denise Marchionda and refuted Davis' claim where he accused me of desecrating my good friend's dead body. On September 16, 2013, Jimmy interviewed my attorney, Marisa Campagna, on the air and followed up by interviewing me on the show on the 17th and 19th.

Communities United Political Action Committee (CUPAC) took notice of the radio discussions and announced that it would be hosting a forum in Dorchester on Friday, September 20, 2013, to discuss the present issues of corruption and discrimination by the leadership of the Boston Police. Davis and I were among those invited to speak at the forum. I had retired in 2010, so there was nothing the Lowell or Boston Police could do to stop me from speaking. I truly hoped Davis would attend, because we were now on equal footing. *The Globe*, *The Herald*, and all the local news stations were invited, but none showed up. Davis did not show either. I, on the other hand, did attend and spoke of the perjury and corruption I saw committed by Davis in Lowell.

I didn't have an actual speech prepared. When I was told it would be a forum, I envisioned more of a panel discussion rather than a straight oral presentation, which caught me off guard. I managed to get my point across though. I brought up Davis' past practices in Lowell, and mentioned Otero and myself as examples of his history of implementing discriminatory policies.

CUPAC filmed the forum and posted it on YouTube (Community Forum Leadership of the Boston Police Department). During the forum, a number of issues concerning Davis were addressed. The speakers pointed out that although Davis was perceived as the Boston Marathon Bombing hero, they said he had actually gone home for the day when it happened, and was really just a media mouthpiece (Community Forum Leadership of the Boston Police Department). They noted that under Davis, the homicide clearance rate in the mostly white community was at 100% while it was less than 50% in communities of color. Davis is good at saying he supports diversity and inclusiveness, but the facts show that he does not. He claimed his command staff was 42% minority, but didn't disclose that they all had to report to a white bureau chief. None of the specialized units in Boston were commanded by officers of color under Davis. He was not promoting officers of color and was trying to blame the civil service test. But, when four officers who had equal marks were up for promotion, only the two white officers were promoted. They also discussed programs that were in place to limit the number of new members of color. It was like Lowell all over again.

The forum was on Friday evening, and on Monday, September 22, 2013, Davis announced he was resigning as the commissioner of the Boston Police. The media never asked or even pondered the question as to why he was resigning. There were just these vague assessments about how he was, "moving on to bigger and better things." The media allowed him to slip away with his hero image intact. At this point, I want to state that I take full responsibility for forcing his resignation. The peasant dethroned the king.

I still was not satisfied. The truth never came out. I was still disgusted that the only news of my lawsuit ever printed was the totally bogus article in the *Lowell Sun* written by Lisa Redmond that depicted me as troubled cop playing the race card. Early in October 2013, I hired Matthew Fogelman, an attorney who focused on defamation cases. Fogelman drafted a letter to the *Lowell Sun* about the way my case had been depicted in the news. A reporter from the *Sun*, Christopher Scott, responded to Fogelman and related that he was now interested in the story and would like to speak with me.

I spoke with Scott on the phone and described in detail the corruption and perjury committed by Davis and his command staff. I pointed out the inaccuracies of Lisa Redmond's so-called news article. Scott never addressed her incompetence. He redirected the blame of the inaccuracies of her article on me for not rebuking her writing at the time it was published. I pointed out specifically that Redmond described the assault and battery by Kennedy as just a "tussle," which seriously downplayed the seriousness of it all. On October 31, 2013, the *Lowell Sun* printed the article, "City Payment to Former Cop: $642,000". Scott never addressed Davis' conduct and labeled the Kennedy assault as a "tussle" again in his writing.

It wasn't much of a step up from Redmond's article, but it did cause a stir with the Lowell city council. Apparently they had absolutely no clue that the city just paid out $642,000 to me because the payout was never put into the budget. Marisa and I gave O'Conner an extra year to make budget accommodations and she did nothing. When the city council began discussing my case, it stated that it should have been settled long ago, and never should have been appealed. The council was puzzled as to the reason why such a case would be appealed in the first place, and why the city's lawyers waited six years to act on it (Hannan).

I wanted to help them find some answers, so I sent emails to some of the city council members explaining that the purpose of the six-year delay was to let the statute of limitations run out in order to protect Davis and his staff from criminal prosecution. Once the council received these emails, it never raised any further questions.

I believe this illustrates the systemic presence and nurturing of police corruption. The city's manager, mayor, and city council all looked the other way or helped perpetuate the corruption because it was beneficial to them in their positions. Davis' protection and promotion of Tommy Kennedy was beneficial to James Kennedy, the city auditor. When a politician needs a favor from the police, it's essential that the request will be honored when needed. Having the police in your pocket is essential for political improprieties that need to go away. A dirty cop in your pocket is always better than a professional cop who functions on principle.

Conclusion

I want to believe that there are professional police departments somewhere in this country. I worked in some that were well run and efficient. There are good cops, and there are good police departments. There are just as many departments that are filled with the type of corruption that I experienced in Lowell, though, and that is not acceptable. Too many police supervisory positions are political and not given based on skill and ability. How do you stop this? If it were an easy answer, I'm sure it would have ended by now.

Stories like my story are important because they can offer a first-hand view of where things have gone wrong, and identify the type of environment where cops like Davis and the other men in this book are made.

One of the biggest problems in police departments today is the predominance of the police "families" that maintain control over police departments. Nepotism is the rule, rather than the exception, when it comes to hiring, promoting, and disciplining officers. This causes the departments to be run on a feudalistic system where officers are placed into categories of royalty and peasant. Family members are royalty, and all others, particularly minorities, are peasants. This system creates an environment of discrimination and racism that is pretty much impossible to avoid and it is perpetuated by a public perception that white officers are superior to minority officers. Often the public is led to believe that minority officers are hired because discrimination laws force departments to hire them, and that white officers with more skill are passed over. This public resentment of the perceived favoritism toward minorities over whites is still prevalent today. Based on this false belief the public then concludes that discrimination against minorities just cannot exist. I think I've presented an abundance of evidence to completely debunk this commonly accepted belief.

The general public has a completely false image of what the police "family" actually is. This is evidenced by TV shows like *Blue Bloods*. In this show, a multi-generational Irish family holds several key positions in the police department, including many command staff level posts. This family is committed to searching out dirty cops in an effort to stop corruption.

The reality is that police families are actually the source of corruption in our police departments today. It is a systemic problem because these families are in leadership positions that perpetuate the corruption. These families are an exclusive subculture that maintain their position through the use of unwritten rules and double standards. These rules utilize lying and cheating as tactics to suppress outsiders (minorities) who threaten or do not accept their dominance. In my case, I did not accept their dominance and had five police chiefs blatantly lie under oath at my trial. The dominance of these police families is the nucleus of the police department. This is the heart and soul of police corruption.

Pedigree is valued over performance. A good example of this is Crowley's rise to team leader on the SWAT team. Based on his performance at Round Up and the fact that he rarely showed up on call outs, he should never have held a leadership position on the team. But he was Davis' golden boy and that was the only "qualification" that he needed. My personal work ethic has always been to let performance speak for itself. Just do the job to the best of your ability and forget about networking. Focus on enhancing personal skill and ability rather than schmoozing. Networking and schmoozing would never have worked for me in the Marines. In Lowell, it's the ultimate strategy for advancement for those who are not in the royalty class.

Realistically, if performance had a place in the hiring and promotion of officers, Lowell could easily operate with far fewer officers than it currently employs. A principled, professional cop wants to work. A principled, professional cop responds to calls because he or she wants to do the job. So many of the connected people in Lowell were there for an easy paycheck; they became cops because they knew they would be taken care of and it would be easy for them to move up in the ranks. They could make easy money while exerting minimal effort, with the bonus of masturbating their ego on the public at the same time.

The idea of community policing is problematic as well. Based on my experience, community policing shouldn't be about having a friendly rapport with the police for that warm, fuzzy feeling or reducing the fear of crime. People do not want or need police officers to be their pals, they don't need officers to play basketball with them, and hand out free ice cream. The public really doesn't care about how Officer Friendly put a reflective sticker on Junior's bicycle. Community policing should be knowing and trusting that when you call the police, the officer who shows up is capable and professional. It's knowing that he'll step into the line of danger to protect you and your family and having confidence that he knows the law and applies it justly and fairly, and is looking out for your best interests.

The citizens want to know that a cop will show up when they call 911 and properly administer CPR when their child is choking. They want to know that someone will quickly respond when they call the police because a man is trying to beat down their door to rape them. They need to know that the men and women in blue are trained to know how effectively to assess when a situation is dangerous so that innocent people are not shot and killed by someone they expect to protect them.

Police officers need to develop and maintain a reputation of honor and justice with the public. To uphold justice, the police must be accountable for their acts, just like citizens are under the law. Cops should be held to the higher standard that is always talked about but never adhered to.

The tactics used under the community policing model is just smoke and mirrors to distract attention away from all the corrupt and unprofessional conduct. Deal honestly with corruption and unprofessional conduct and then there will be no need for community policing.

The lie of community policing is an expensive one. Davis received millions of dollars to implement community policing programs, yet the city of Lowell was listed as the eighteenth most dangerous city in the United States in 2011 (Goldman). All that money wasted. Professionalism and accountability are free. If the focus were there, the public would save all the tax dollars dumped into community policing grants.

Presently politicians and police chiefs continue to turn to community policing as a credible tactic to reduce crime. After Davis announced his resignation, a news article entitled, "Boston Police Chief Ed Davis: Fight Terrorism like Crime," was published. In the article,Davis is quoted as saying that "a key to preventing future attacks like the Boston marathon bombing is to bring crime fighting community policing strategies to the battle against terrorism."

Really? Community policing is going to stop terrorism? Community policing has not had an effect on lowering crime and now it's going to stop terrorism? Davis stated that community policing was already being utilized in Boston under his command, so why didn't it stop the marathon bombing? The article also quotes Davis as saying that "he knew immediately when he arrived on the scene that the twin explosions were terrorist acts - and he has been trained that Al Qaeda hits in three attacks."

Three attacks? This is such a simplistic and ignorant statement. He seems to be referring to the 9/11 attacks where the Twin Towers and the Pentagon were hit. Except there were actually four teams of terrorist hijackers. He forgot flight 93 never made it to its target in Washington and was downed in Pennsylvania. This type of talk keeps getting fed to the public and it has to stop. The D.A.R.E. program (Drug Abuse Resistance Education) which enjoyed years of funding has now been overall determined to be ineffective by several sources. It is now a generally accepted belief that D.A.R.E. has failed and Community policing needs to be accepted as a failure also and stop the lying.

There is also the issue of police officers killing unarmed or innocent people. I was placed in a number of situations where I could have easily and justifiably killed people and claimed self-defense. You can't just kill people when the situation skirts a deadly force scenario and then fall on the standard defense that "I was in fear for my life." If you are that fucking afraid, find another line of work. There is a difference between a split second life-and-death decision, and going directly to deadly force because you lack the strength or skill or mental capacity to deal with the situation.

In 1990, when Operation Desert Shield was underway, I tried to get back in the Marines and I had gotten as far as my physical when Desert Storm was completed in January 1991. I believe I would have no issue with killing in combat. But as a police officer, the rules of engagement are completely different. An infantry Marine's job is to kill, a police officer's job is to protect. The deadly force scenarios in which I was involved were mostly dealing with suicidal people who displayed poor fighting or weapons skill. Subduing them and taking them alive was always the ultimate goal and what I thought was the true sign of a professional.

The country needs the police to perform at the highest level of professionalism. But what we often see is a mediocre performance under stress, where the system protects them and justifies their conduct. They need to know when their lives are really in danger, and they can't let fear overtake them. I've seen so many people come on the job who absolutely lack the capacity to handle routine police work proficiently. For them to function at a higher level of discipline in a deadly force incident would be greatly in doubt. We live in a violent world and if you're going to be a cop and actually work the street, it's reasonable to believe that at some point your life will be in danger. When it does happen, it shouldn't come as this huge surprise. What did you think you were signing up for?

But once they are on the job and show they lack the ability they can't be weeded out. The female police officer who made detective because she was scared should have stayed on the street and been supervised. Document her incompetence. If she can't do the job, ask for a resignation or fire her. Don't promote her to a specialty position. Put professionals in the criminal bureau, not pawns. But you can't do that because it looks sexist and there may be a civil lawsuit. There was no fear of me filing a lawsuit, but with this female they are afraid. It's better to keep her because they now own her and it maintains the facade of inclusiveness. I'm using this female as an example, but there are plenty of men who fit into this category as well.

The rampant discrimination also needs to be addressed. Minorities are tolerated as long as they don't want to move up and acknowledge their place as peasants. If you're a "good" minority you may receive a "gift" of a specialty position as a detective or instructor. Specialty positions are gifted rather than earned through job performance. This culture of superiority over lesser officers is blatantly displayed inside the police department, while an image of equality is projected to the general public. This attitude of superiority spills over into the way officers deal with the public and is one of the causes behind the numerous unprovoked police shootings and killings that occur more and more frequently in the United States today.

I've heard arguments from cops that the cases Otero and I brought against the city weren't based on racial discrimination because white guys who were innocent received excessive punishment under Davis as well. John Leary was fired for having a verbal argument with an ex-girlfriend. Scotty Fuller was charged with sexual harassment with no victim, along with Otero. Gerry Flynn was charged with swearing and conduct unbecoming. Franky Nobrega was bypassed for promotion because Davis heard rumors about him. These guys are white and were wrongly punished by Davis as well. Flynn and Fuller's positions contributed to Davis' motivation in targeting them. Who knows what happened with the others.

First and foremost, I believe Davis is dirty and corrupt; there is no denying that. But I think Davis is also clearly a racist and his actions are discriminatory. Rivera, Pender, and the Otero brothers all were Hispanic and held no opposing or antagonistic position against Davis. The only thing going against Angel Otero was he was Hispanic and next to be promoted.

The way Davis punished me and protected Kennedy is so blatantly discriminatory that I can't begin to conceptualize how someone can fool themselves into believing that racism played no role. But what completely solidifies the existence of racial discrimination is the fact that minority officers in Boston echoed the same incidents of disparate treatment by Davis that I witnessed in Lowell. The discrimination in Lowell was not an isolated incident.

Another systemic problem in the police forces of today is the extensive use of lying, especially by command staff and police families. The media has coined the phrase, "the code of silence," but it should be "the code of lying." There is no need to develop skill or experience if you can just lie. One example that is particularly infuriating was when Cormier changed official police reports for his friend to prevent him from receiving an OUI. This is an obstruction of justice and he should have been fired. Instead he received a slap on the wrist.

These men and women are often able to say just that they have the necessary skill and it is passed off as true. Lying is an abuse of the freedom of speech outlined in the First Amendment. They turn the freedom of the First Amendment from a benevolent humanitarian granting of expression into a tool used to oppress the innocent and perpetuate corruption. I have vigorously fought for justice and most of the systems in place to uphold justice have fallen short.

Additionally, these men and women are not subject to the same type of discipline as minority officers, which I feel I have demonstrated numerous times throughout my story. In my case, I think the system and its accompanying institutions failed to do the basic functions for which they were originally created.

The institutions that I attempted to utilize throughout my fight did not serve their purpose, and that is not okay. These institutions were created for a reason and they should remain true to their purpose. Police corruption will continue to thrive as long as these institutions continue to fail to perform their function.

The police union should exist to protect officers from wrongful prosecution by police and city administrations. Although I received legal assistance, I was ultimately betrayed and given false legal advice that only aided Davis and the city.

The city manager's hearing, where the purpose is to review the elements of the police department's fairness of the issuance of discipline, failed to perform its function. The manager Brian Martin completely failed me and the city. If he had honestly done his job, the case would have ended there. I would have had a chance to have a career and the city would have been saved $642,000, plus the cost of hundreds of hours for city attorneys to defend this case.

Civil Service was supposed to provide a fair and impartial hearing of the facts and determine a fair and just finding. The testimony presented completely cleared me of any wrongdoing, yet they found I was not credible. I was found to be the liar amongst all the lying presented.

I feel like turning to MCAD for assistance was a complete waste of time. I don't know why this organization even exists, other than to suck up tax dollars. Supposedly, MCAD's whole purpose is to address cases like mine. This would have been a hallmark case for their organization. In all seriousness, MCAD should be disbanded and the building in the center of Boston should be rented out for something that will create cash flow rather than the deficit it creates. My disappointment with MCAD is beyond profound.

The civil lawsuit in front of a jury of my peers contained no peers. Although I won, the winning was weak and no discrimination was found, even though the preponderance of evidence was clearly proven. You can surmise that even when discrimination is clearly and boldly displayed to white people, their predominant belief that discrimination doesn't exist will override the facts with which they are faced.

To be fair, a lot of white people have never really experienced discrimination. Until you have experienced it up close and personal, either through a close friend's experience, or somehow experiencing life as a minority themselves, I don't think even the most well-meaning person can truly understand what it is like to be discriminated against. I am half-white, and I don't mean to rail against white people necessarily. But I have come against negativity based on my ethnic appearance for my whole life, in grade school all the way up to the present day. If you have not lived in that reality, you will really struggle to understand it. Walking a mile in someone else's shoes is often easier said than done. That is why I felt that the jury, in my case, was not truly a jury of my peers. They had good intentions, and they tried to be fair. But they could not really understand what it was like to be discriminated against because they had most likely never experienced it.

The only institution that actually performed its function was the Appeals Court. The Appeals Court judges clearly looked at the evidence through a methodical unbiased application of the law and came to the conclusion that I completely provided the evidence necessary for the charges I filed and determined that police officials provided false testimony.

Throughout my whole experience, there was no mechanism available to me to chastise or punish officials who blatantly lied. Lying by police officials was acceptable conduct throughout and none of them were ever admonished for their conduct. Each one of them has continued to have a prosperous career. Lying appears to be an acceptable tactic used by law enforcement to win cases. It appears it's my job, as the complainant, to irrefutably expose their false evidence as the only method to prevail. The overall attitude is, "ok you won. It's over, move along. Let's get to the next case." Clearly there are straightforward criminal cases where there is honest and clear testimony with true evidence for convictions. But there are also cases where the police possess vindictive and malicious motivations. For these cases, lying is the tactic utilized to achieve victory. Lying takes no effort. Disproving the lie takes tremendous time and effort. Maybe, in the next case, the complainant and/or defendant can effectively expose the lie. If not, they lose.

The role of police is to enforce the law and protect the people though the application of the principles of honesty, integrity and bravery. The police families hide behind this image, and the ugly truth is that these issues, this system, and the culture that it promotes is unlikely to change. How can things change for the better if politicians continue to overlook corruption because it serves their purpose? As long as the media and Hollywood prop up men like Davis and portray them as heroes, innocent people will continue to be convicted and go to jail. Innocent people will continue to be shot. Cops like me will go nowhere and be forced off the job or submit to corruption. You can't be a man in an old-boy system. The way things are now, dirty cops can rise to stardom through lying and cheating and it is futile for honest police officers to even try.

The reality of what happens behind the scenes is one that the public doesn't know about. Hopefully, I have given you a better glimpse into that dark reality. I can't candy coat this shit and give you a rainbow at the end. I wish I could. The system is so entrenched, I don't think it can ever be fixed. For dirty cops like Davis and the politicians who support the corruption, there is no motivation to change. They are in power and they want to keep it. They aren't going to all of a sudden become ethical and principled for no reason.

It appears that many young cops come on the job with the best of intentions, but those good intentions are quickly diminished once they become engulfed in the true essence of animus that is the police world. A lot of cops are just beaten down by this reality and try to exist void of their original optimistic ideals. My method of survival was to embrace my principles with a much greater devotion than I had in the past. I firmly believed that truth and justice would be mine as long I continued to believe in these powerful concepts that are the basis of our democracy, when face-to-face, truth and justice will always prevail over lying and cheating. I would utilize the criminal justice systems and laws as they were designed to be used and I would prevail.

I was powerless in a massive system that was focused on my demise. All I had was my own personal integrity to draw upon. Yes, foolishly optimistic, but it got me through it all. Although I never obtained the positions and career I sought, I achieved goals that were within my reach. I retired with my pension and won back something to make up for what I lost. And, ultimately, from my powerless position, I forced a powerful and corrupt chief of police to resign. In that respect, I wasn't powerless. Davis controlled the police department, the union, civil service, and the media, and he was labeled a national hero. The only power I had was my integrity and the truth. This benign power source was enough to take Davis out in the long run.

I stood alone through this whole odyssey. If one or maybe two other people showed some character and stood up for what was right, this story would have been much shorter. In a way, this is a call to arms for anyone with a badge on their chest and a national ensign on their sleeve to step up and show some honor. Individual integrity is your source of power. As more cops step up, that power will grow exponentially. The only way things can change for the better is for the rank-and-file patrolmen to stay true to their oath and pursue their careers with integrity. Benevolent change will only come from the bottom up, not the top down. You can't look to politicians and police chiefs for any leadership. Only if cops remain steadfast in their core principles will they be able to reach any level of honor. I was taught that the generals don't win the battles, it's the efforts of the grunts on the battlefield that win the war. In the war against police corruption, individual officers who stand up for what is right will be the ones who will prevail.

Where Are They Now?

Currently the movie *Patriot's Day* is scheduled to be released in December 2016 about the Boston Marathon Bombing. Ed Davis is to be portrayed by John Goodman, again as a hero. To this day, no one has been willing to pick up the story of his past and look at it from a reasonable standpoint. I am not the only one who has accused Ed Davis of corrupt and discriminatory practices, he has a long list of people he has treated offensively. The true heroes of the Boston Marathon Bombing should be celebrated, not a man who has built his career on lies and deceit.

Additionally, Davis has opened his own private security company where he advises major companies in their security programs and procedures. He is a fellow at Harvard University's John Hopkins institution, and he uses his credentials in law enforcement and his ties to academia to promote his business. He works with clients like the Boston Red Sox, Uber, WBC Channel 4, and the *Boston Globe* as a security consultant. His career has continued to thrive. Davis has used lying as the main instrument to propel his career and it's worked well for him, so he has no motivation to stop.

Even recently, he has lied in the media. On May 5, 2016, Megan Wells of PoliceOne.com wrote:

"Shortly after the bombing occurred, Commissioner Davis went on the record saying that apart from combat during his overseas deployment, the bombing incident (and carnage) was unlike anything he'd seen."

A very courageous statement indeed. The only problem is Davis never served in any branch of the military, hence he was never deployed overseas and never saw combat. He was hired on in Lowell in 1978 when he was 22 years old, and worked there until 2006 when he went to Boston. He has never known anything other than police work in a very small section of the United States for his entire career.

Davis had triple bypass heart surgery in his late forties. He is a large man and a physical mess. The man can hardly walk trying to carry his obese mass around. He was clearly unfit to serve during the Iraq and Afghanistan wars. After the release of *Patriot's Day*, maybe Wahlberg can make another movie all about Davis' combat tour. There would have to be an extensive use of computer generated imagery (CGI).

Kennedy still works as an officer in Lowell. He is currently a Captain and was fourth in line for Chief a few years ago. He was not chosen, ultimately someone decided Billy Taylor was a better choice for the job. On April 4, 2015, Kennedy was working a bar detail, where he offered an intoxicated woman a ride in his unmarked take-home cruiser. He left his assignment with this woman and headed to a nearby parking lot. At some point, Kennedy's conduct forced this woman to bolt from his cruiser and she walked four blocks to the police station to file a formal complaint. An investigation was conducted and he received a five-day suspension that will be removed from his file in a year. This way he can continue to be promoted. The suspension was for leaving his post, as the investigation conveniently didn't discover any indecent sexual assault, despite the woman's claims (Scott 2015). The police department didn't find anything wrong with his conduct, but apparently his wife did because she threw him out and he ended up living back with his parents.

Buckley works in the family services unit as a domestic violence officer in Lowell. Crowley is next in line to be chief, and Demoura became the chief of police in Fitchburg, Massachusetts.

Lavallee became chief after Davis transferred to Boston; and when he left, Captain Taylor was chosen to take his place. Taylor has a long history of alcoholism. In 2008, he was found unconscious with his service weapon in his department-issued take home cruiser at a soccer field in Lowell. He was transported to the hospital by ambulance for an alcohol overdose. He attended an alcohol rehab before returning to work, and received no other discipline.

Stanley was chief of two towns at one point, Wareham and North Andover. During his career as chief, he received a drunk driving charge. That didn't slow down his career either.

Eileen Donahue, the former mayor, is now a Massachusetts Senator representing the Middlesex district.

All of the officers at the felony car stop I directed in 1997 were promoted except me. Jack Davis became a Sergeant, Crawford became a Lieutenant, and Leavitt became a Sergeant.

Works Cited

Alvarez, Robert. Lowell Police Dept. Crime/Incident Report. Lowell, MA; LPD PCT1, 13 Apr. 1997. Print.

Appeals Court Finding, Alvarez vs. Lowell. December 21, 2011. Retrieved from http://alvarezvslowellcom.ipage.com/wp-content/uploads/2014/05/FIL676.pdf.

Anderson, T. (2013, August 7). Minority officers call for Edward Davis's Resignation. The Boston Globe. Retrieved from https://www.bostonglobe.com/metro/2013/08/06/minority-officers-group-calls-for-police-commissioner-edward-davis-resign/3Hi3Luw4j31Z6JTlfdh8QK/story.html

Brodey, Sam. 2014, October 23). SWAT teams keep killing innocent people in their homes. Mother Jones, Retrieved from http://www.motherjones.com/politics/2014/10/swat-raid-casualties.

Buckley, Mark. Lowell Police Dept. Crime/Incident Report. Lowell, MA; LPD PCT1, 13 Apr. 1997. Print.

Buckley, Mark. Lowell Police Dept. Crime/Incident Report. Lowell, MA; LPD PCT1, 18 Apr. 1997. Print.

Butterfield, F. (1987, February 8). Ex-policeman Tells of Boston Test Thefts. The New York Times, Retrieved from http://www.nytimes.com/1987/02/08/us/ex-policeman-tells-of-boston-test-thefts.html.

Chestnut v. City of Lowell, 2002 WL 483557 (1st Cir. (Mass.))

Cramer, Maria. "Hub police show no gain in solving homicides." Boston Globe, Date missing, p. A1 and A8.

Cramer, Maria. "Police head defends role after wrongful imprisonment." Boston Globe, Date missing, p. unknown and B5.

Crawford, Donny. Lowell Police Dept. Crime/Incident Report. Lowell, MA; LPD PCT1, unknown. Print.

Congressman Martin Meehan. Meehan Honors Lowell Police for Crime Reduction Efforts and Reminds Bush of His Lack of Support for "COPS" Program. 2001. Web. 8 March 2004. http://www.house.gov/apps/list/press/ma05_meehan/NR_07_30_01crimerel.html.

"Community Forum Leadership of the Boston Police Department." YouTube, uploaded by Touch 106.1 FM, 20 September 2013, https://www.youtube.com/watch?v=u0QZaMLNOho.

Davis, Ed. Dep. 7 April 2000. Alvarez v. City of Lowell. Docket No. 99132814.

Davis, Jack. Lowell Police Dept. Crime/Incident Report. Lowell, MA; LPD PCT1, 18 Apr. 1997. Print.

Estes, Andrea. "Lowell chief said to lead list for Hub commissioner." Boston Globe, Date missing, p. B4.

Fargen, J. and Gelzinis P. (2009, September 27). Thin blue lie. BostonHerald.com. Retrieved from http://www.bostonherald.com/news/regional/view.bg?articleid=1200319&formal=text.

Goldman, L. (2011, May 23). The 25 most dangerous cities in America. Business Insider.

Retrieved from http://www.businessinsider.com/most-dangerous-cities-2011-5#18-lowell-mass-8

Hannan, E. (2013, Nov. 13). Lynch blasted for not sharing info on discrimination appeal with Council. Lowell Sun, (Lowell, MA). Retrieved from http://www.lowellsun.com/news/ci_24512719/lynch-blasted-not-sharing-info-discrimination-appeal-council.

Healey Commission Report. (2004, April 5). The Governor's Commission on Criminal Justice Innovation Critiqued. Criminal Justice Policy Coalition. Retrieved from http://www.cjpc.org/pr_healey_comm_report.htm.

Holland, Adam. "Officers save choking boy." Lowell Sun [Lowell, MA], 13 December 2004, p. 1 and 4.

Kennedy, D. (1987, June 14). Crooked Cops Leave a Tangled Legacy in Cheating Scandal. The Associated Press, Retrieved from http://www.apnewsarchive.com/1987/Crooked-Cops-Leave-a-Tangled-Legacy-in-Cheating-Scandal/id-301757cc5490b3c54c0bd67eefbb2416.

Kennedy, Tom. Lowell Police Dept. Crime/Incident Report. Lowell, MA; LPD PCT1, 12 Apr. 1997. Print.

Kneebone, Elizabeth and Steven Raphael. (2011, May 26). City and Suburban Crime Trends in Metropolitan America. Brookings Press. Retrieved from https://www.brookings.edu/research/city-and-suburban-crime-trends-in-metropolitan-america/.

Lafleur, Michael. "Burden of Proof." Lowell Sun [Lowell, MA], Date missing, p. 9 and 12.

Leavitt, Richard. Lowell Police Dept. Crime/Incident Report. Lowell, MA; LPD PCT11, 18 Apr. 1997. Print.

McCabe, Katie. (2011 Jan. 15). Interview: Betty-Anne Waters, the story behind CONVICTION. The Hollywood News. Retrieved from http://www.thehollywoodnews.com/2011/01/15/interview-betty-anne-watersthe-story-conviction/.

Mehegan, Julie. "Lowell police chief on new crime commission." Boston Globe, Date and page missing.

Mike Laub's Website. Governor's Commission on Criminal Justice Innovation. http://myclob.pbworks.com/w/page/21957818/Governor%E2%80%99s%20Commission%20on%20Criminal%20Justice%20Innovation. Accessed October 10, 2016.

Minch, J. (2001, December 14). City councillor calls for probe into police clerk. LowellSun.com, Retrieved from http://www.lowellsun.com/Stories/0,1002,4761%7E276176,00.html.

Moraff, C. (2016, May 6). The promise and failure of community policing. The Philly Declaration. Retrieved from https://phillydeclaration.org/2015/05/06/the-promise-and-failure-of-community-policing/.

Munsi, S. (2012, June 11). Peoria police officer who posted Obama's image on Facebook appeals demotion. AZCentral. Retrieved from http://archive.azcentral.com/community/peoria/articles/20120611peoria-officer-obama-image-facebook-appeals-demotion.html.

My Plainview. (2002, September 13). Union offers to pay $10,000 to defend police chief against perjury charge. *MyPlainview.com*. Retrieved from http://www.myplainview.com/news/article/Union-offers-to-pay-10-000-to-defend-police-8942678.php

Nadeau R. (2009, September 29). BPD's lying ban sits well. BostonHerald.com. Retrieved from http://www.bostonherald.com/news/regional/view.bg?articleid=1200723&format=text.

Office of the Inspector General. Cops Report Findings and Recommendations by Location. Audit Report 99-14 - Appendix I Continued. https://www.oig.justice.gov/reports/COPS/a9914/9914a12.htm. Accessed 6 October, 2016.

Office of the Inspector General. September 2005. Use of equitable sharing assets by the police department of the city of Lowell, Massachusetts. Audit Report GR-70-05-018. https://www.oig.justice.gov/grants/g7005018.htm. Accessed 6 October, 2016.

Palta, Rina. (2013, December 31). 5 explanations for the great crime decline in Los Angeles and the US. KPCC (Pasadena, CA). Retrieved from http://www.scpr.org/news/2013/12/31/41291/five-explanations-for-the-great-crime-decline-in-l/.

Rezendes, Michael. (2014, Sept. 19). Feds probe use of informants in Lowell. Boston Globe. Retrieved from https://www.bostonglobe.com/metro/2014/09/18/attorney-ortiz-investigating-alleged-lowell-police-misconduct-drug-cases/DAOigsOvcUwJv2y4X4wJHP/story.html.

Rivera et al v. Lowell Police Department. D-6265, 6274, 6266. Commonwealth of Massachusetts Civil Service Commission. 11 Jan. 2001.

Robert Alvarez v. City of Lowell, 2006, MICV 2002-4841 (Middlesex Superior Court (Mass.))

Saccheti, Maria and Matt Viser. (2013, August 1). Boston Police Commissioner Ed Davis is subject of buzz for top homeland security post. *Boston.com.* Retrieved from http://archive.boston.com/politicalintelligence/2013/08/01/boston-police-commissioner-davis-subject-buzz-for-top-homeland-security-post/7qHoyQVg-4DRv85PeYunRzI/story.html

Scott, Christopher. "Why hasn't Cormier been suspended?" Lowell Sun [Lowell, MA], Date and page missing.

Scott, Christopher. "Fall-out from civil service decision." Lowell Sun [Lowell, MA], February 3, 2000, p. 9, 11.

Scott, Christopher. (2013, April 13). Lowell informant probe moves to Essex DA. Lowell Sun [Lowell, MA] Retrieved from http://www.lowellsun.com/ci_23018612/lowell-informant-probe-moves-essex-da?IADID=Search-www.lowellsun.com-www.lowellsun.com&IADID=Search-www.lowellsun.com-www.lowellsun.com.

Scott, Christopher. (2013, October 31). City payout to former cop: $642,000. Lowell Sun [Lowell, MA] Retrieved from http://blogs.lowellsun.com/thecolumn/2013/10/31/city-payout-to-former-cop-642000/

Scott, Christopher. (2015, August 21). Lowell Police Capt. Kennedy punished for conduct 'unbecoming an officer'. Lowell Sun [Lowell, MA] Retrieved from http://www.lowellsun.com/news/ci_28680931/.

Schieder, Matthew. (2008, January). Community Policing Nugget: Community Policing Defined. Community Policing Dispatch. Vol. 1, Issue 1. Retrieved from http://cops.usdoj.gov/html/dispatch/january_2008/nugget.html.

Skruck, J. (2001, December 13). Police clerk in shoplifting case resigns. LowellSun.com, Retrieved from http://www.lowellsun.com/Stories/0,1002,4761%&E273382,00.html

Thacher, David. National Cops Evaluation Organizational Change Case Study: Lowell, Massachusetts. John F. Kennedy School of Government. Harvard University. Retrieved from https://www.ncjrs.gov/nij/cops_casestudy/lowell4.html.

"Thirty Years After Wrongful Conviction: Reflections from Exoneree Dennis Maher." YouTube, uploaded by BC Law, 9 April 2014, https://www.youtube.com/watch?v=wtcLminoBns.

United States Department of Justice. Community Oriented Policing Services About Page. http://www.cops.usdoj.gov/Default.asp?Item=35. Accessed 6 October, 2016.

Unknown. (1994, May 16). Police mistakes cited in death of Boston man. The New York Times, Retrieved from http://www.nytimes.com/1994/05/16/us/police-mistakes-cited-in-death-of-boston-man.html.

Unknown. (2000, September 7). Attorney General Janet Reno announces $1 million in grants for "Police as problem solvers and peacemakers initiative". US Department of Justice Community Oriented Policing Services. Retrieved from http://cops.usdoj.gov/default.asp?Item=531.

Unknown. "Globe reporters to write book on bombings." Boston Globe, 26 May 2013, p. B12.

Vanessa Dixon v. Lowell Retirement Board. CR-08-259 (DALA, 2008). Retrieved from http://www.mass.gov/anf/hearings-and-appeals/decisions/gen-jurisdiction-decisions/c-d/vanessa-dixon-v-lowell-retirement-board.html.

Vibes, John. (2016, Feb. 21). Cops caught forcing scientists to falsify DNA tests to get more prosecutions - now they're furious. The Free Thought Project. Retrieved from http://www.cbsnews.com/news/annie-dookhan-chemist-at-mass-crime-lab-arrested-for-allegedly-mishandling-over-60000-samples/.

Wells, M. (2016, May 5). Hollywood to tell the Boston Marathon Bombing story from a first responder's perspective. PoliceOne.com. Retrieved from https://www.policeone.com/entertainment/articles/178527006-Hollywood-to-tell-the-Boston-Marathon-Bombing-story-from-a-first-responders-perspective/.

Wickenheiser, Matt. "Ruling: City had no firm evidence against 4 officers accused in sex harassment on bus." Lowell Sun [Lowell, MA], February 2, 2000, p. unknown and 12.

Wilson, Reid. (2015, January 2). In major cities, murder rates drop precipitously. The Washington Post. Retrieved from https://www.washingtonpost.com/blogs/govbeat/wp/2015/01/02/in-major-cities-murder-rates-drop-precipitously/.